PICTURE BOOK OF CALMING SCENES

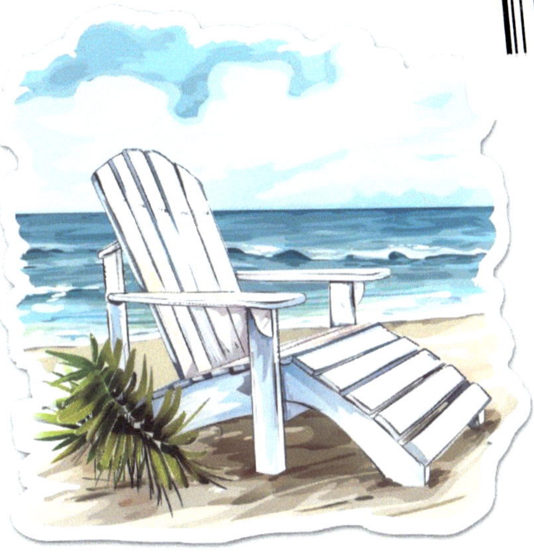

...By...

Ella Caldwell

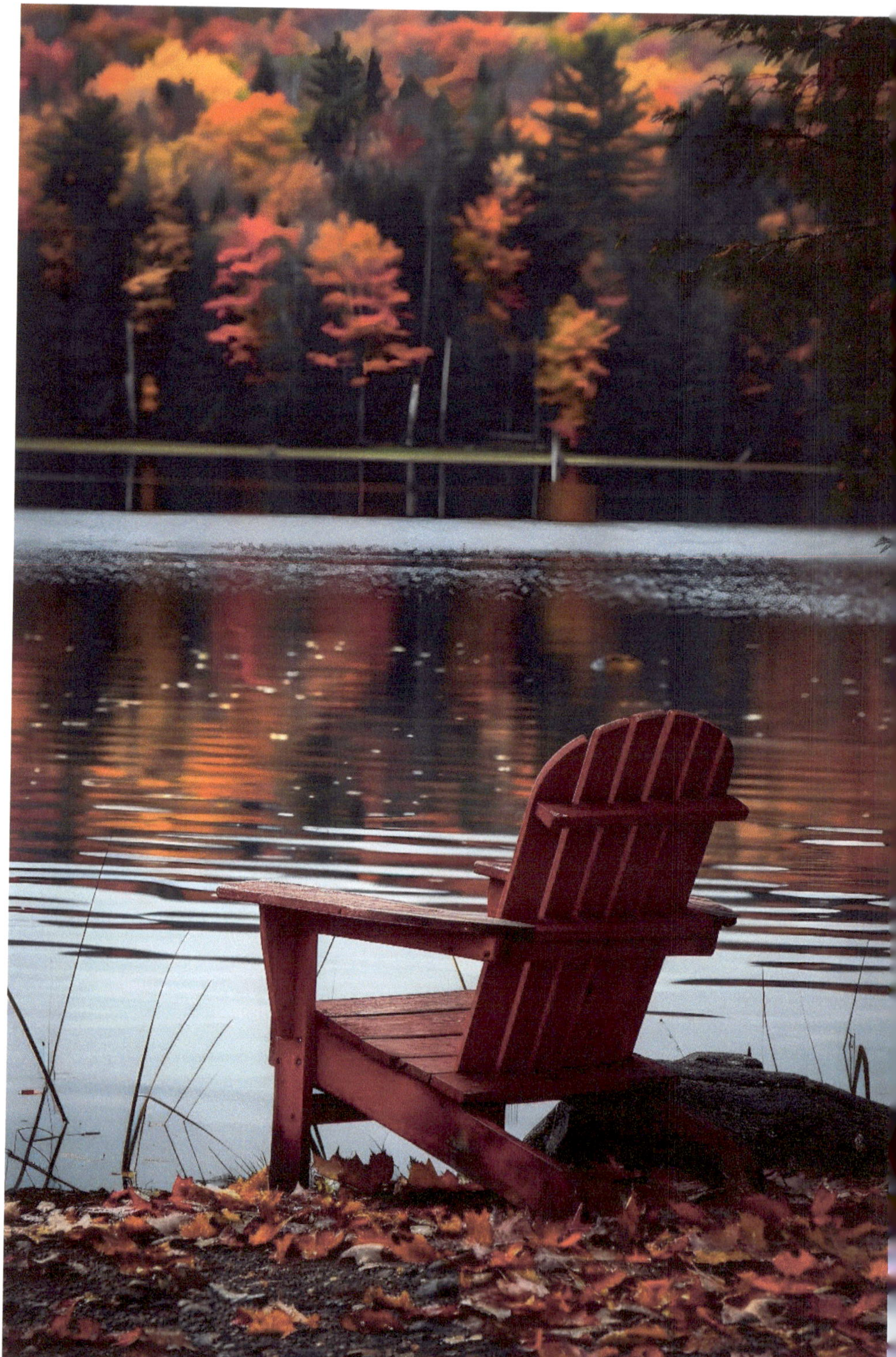

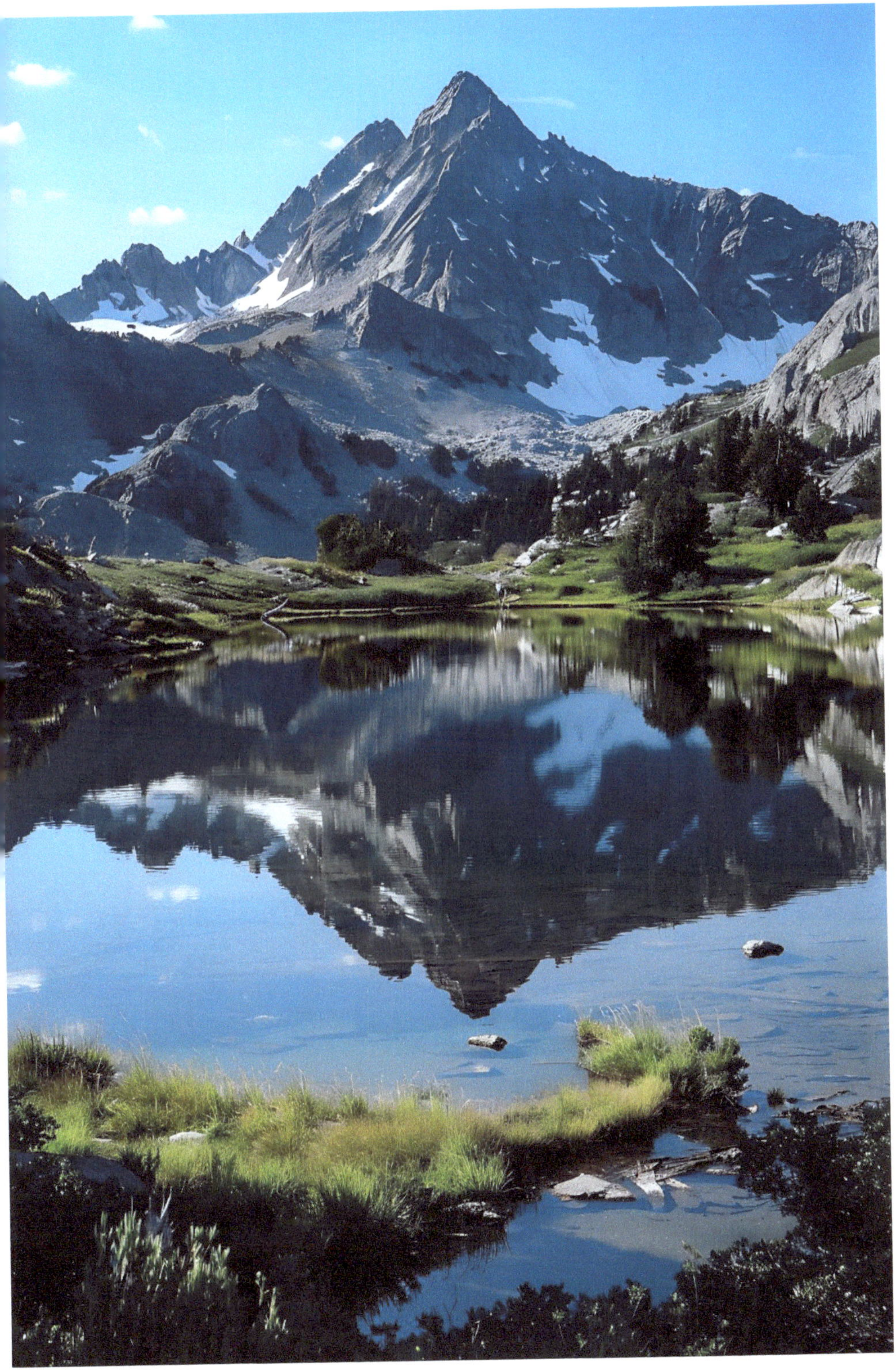

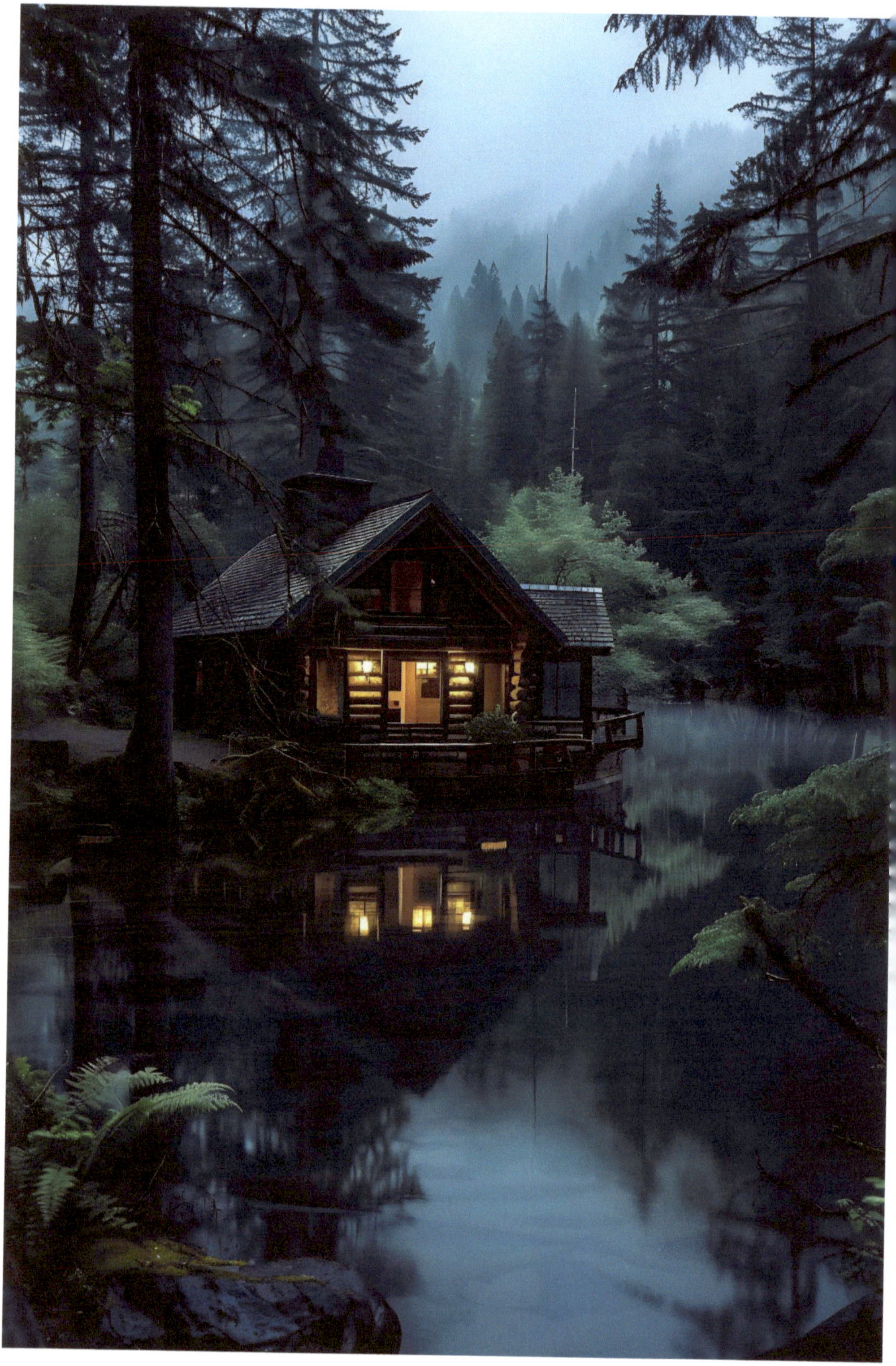

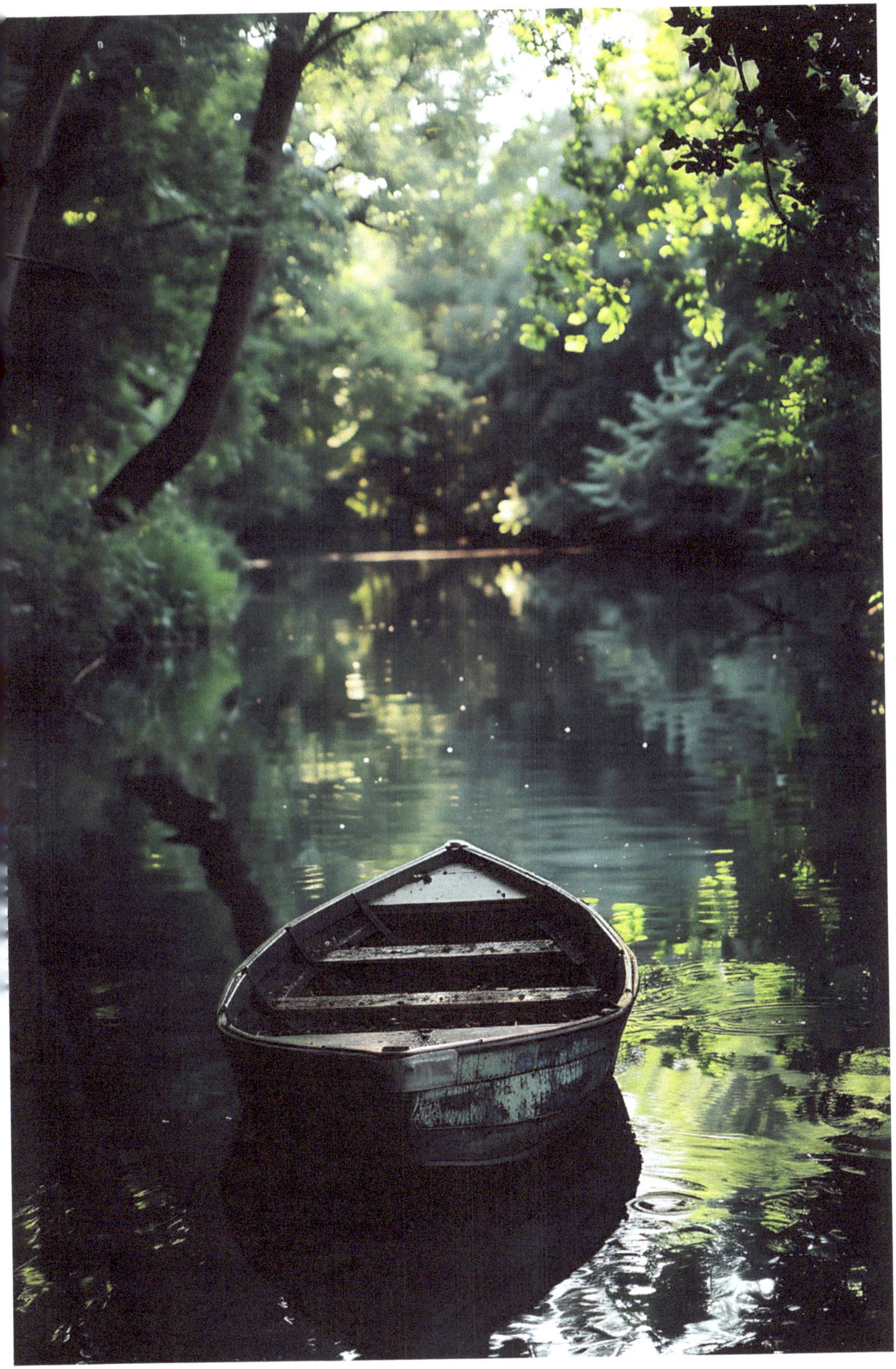

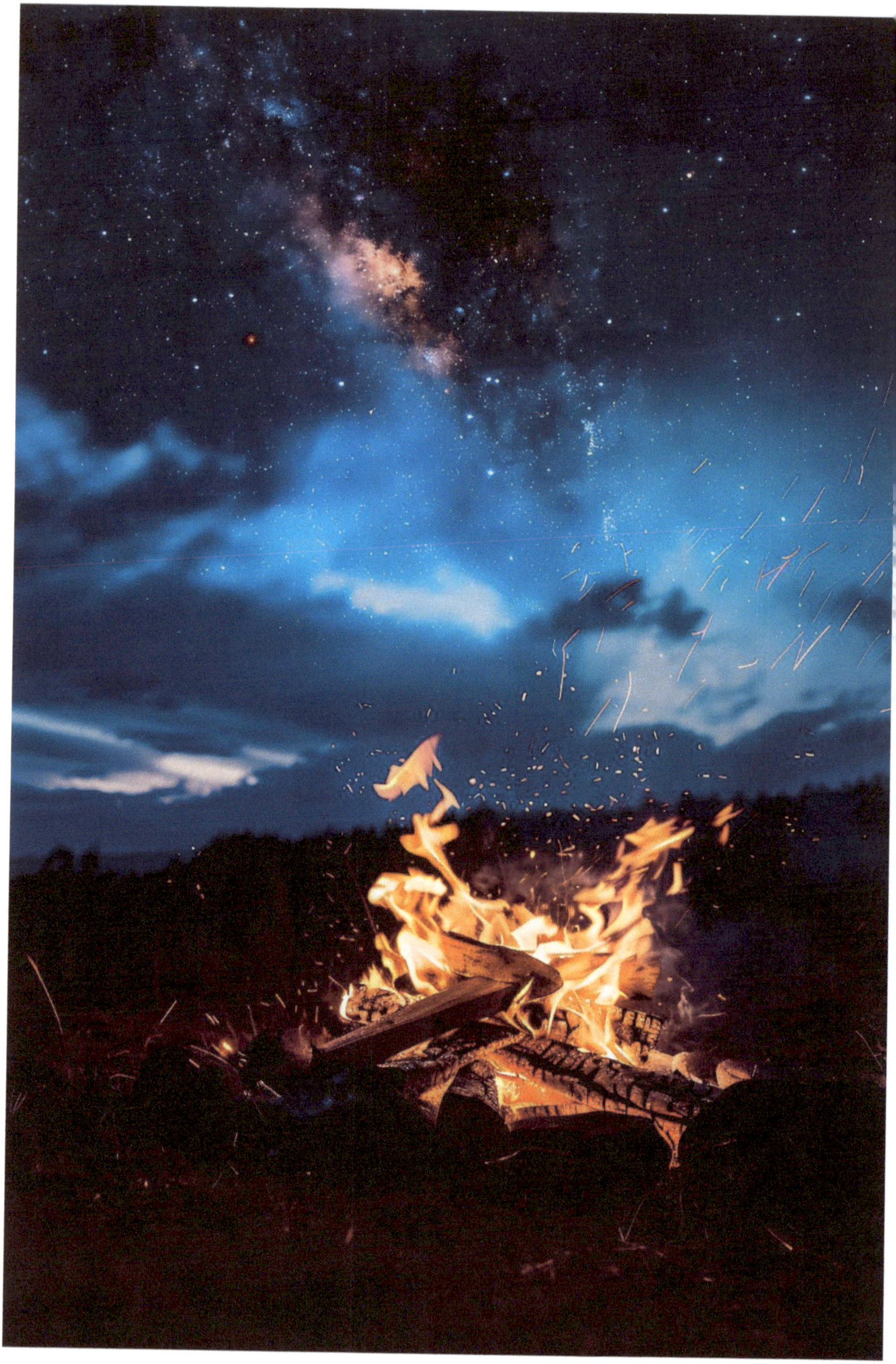

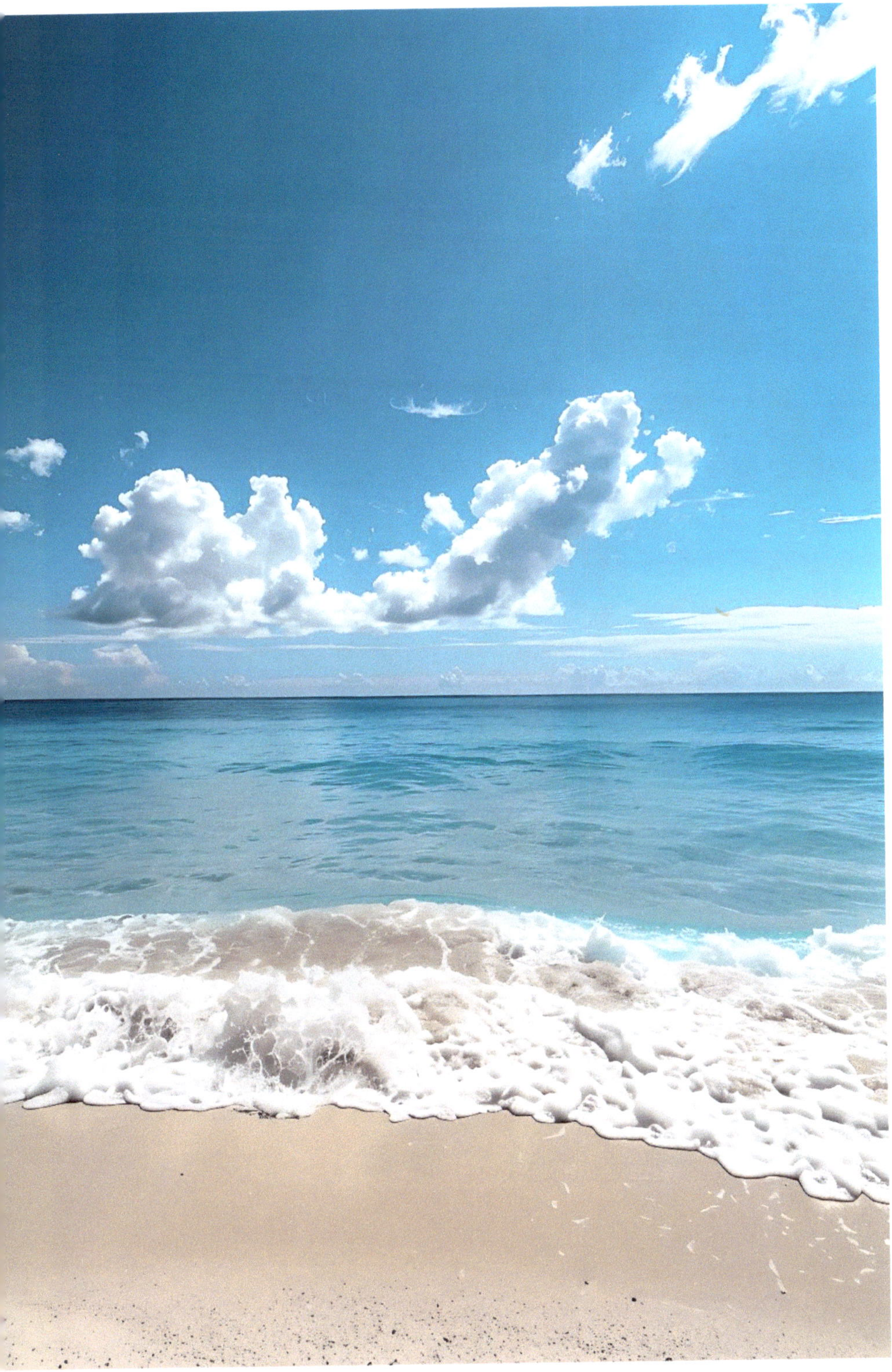

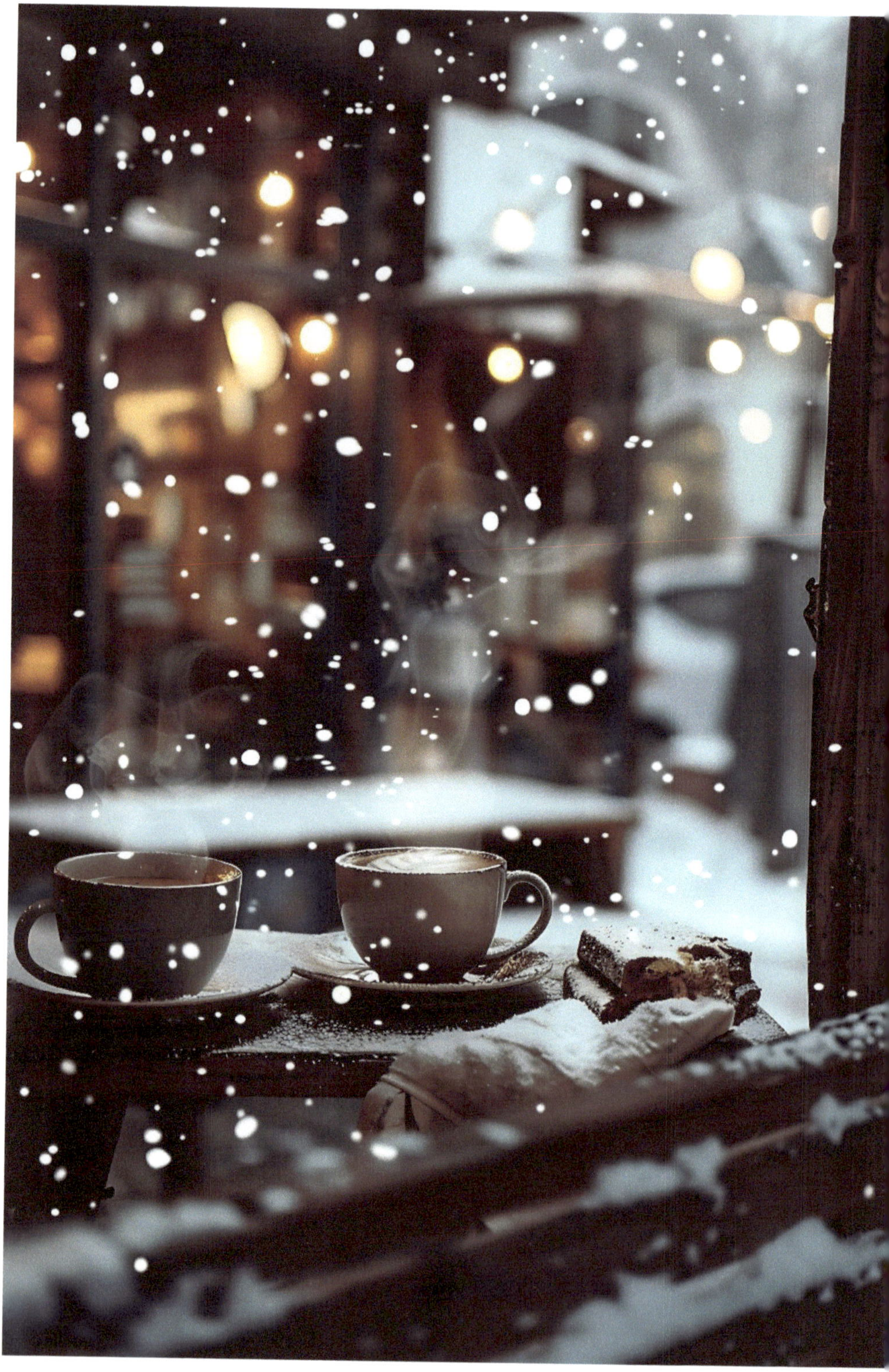

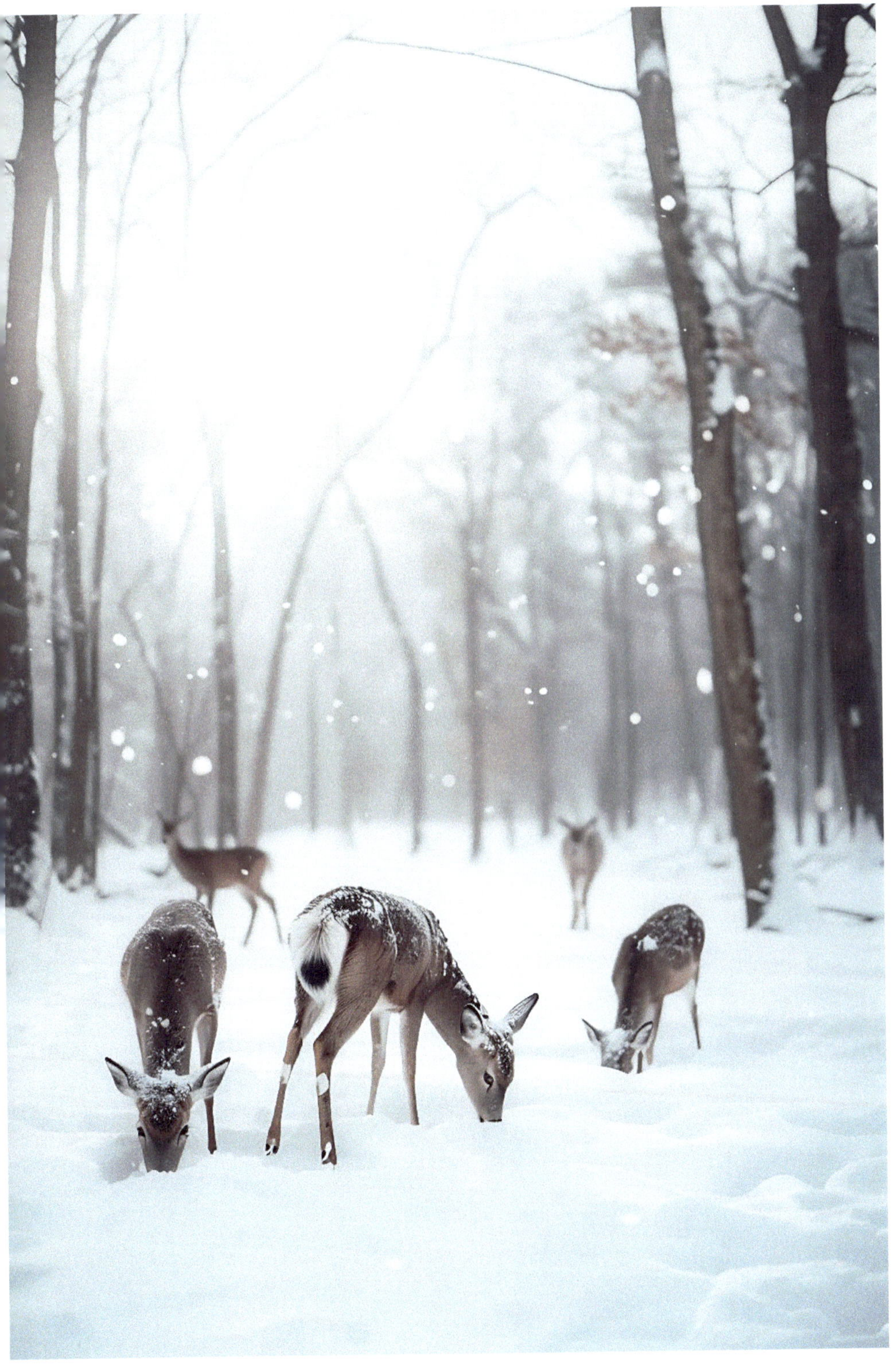

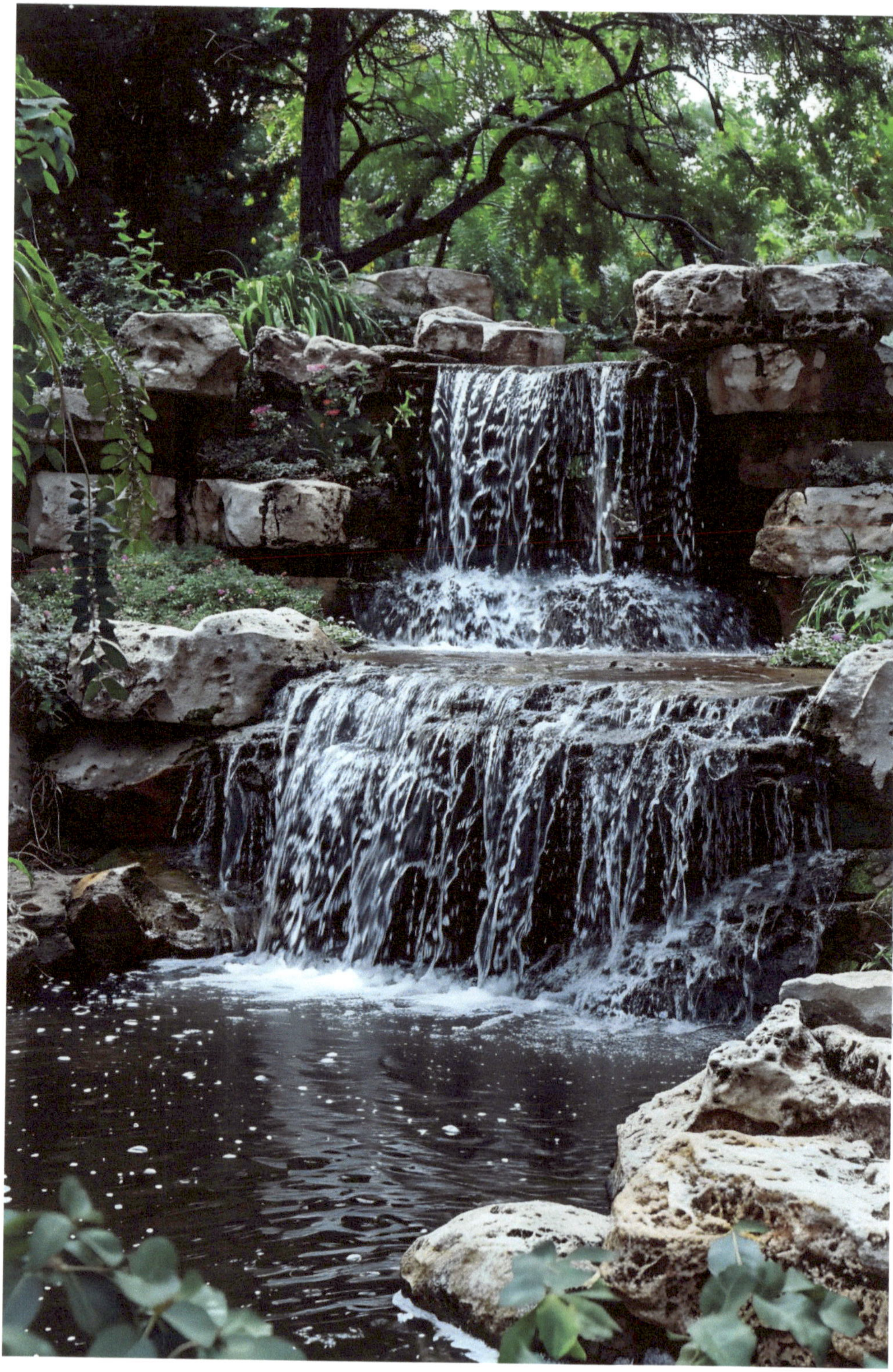

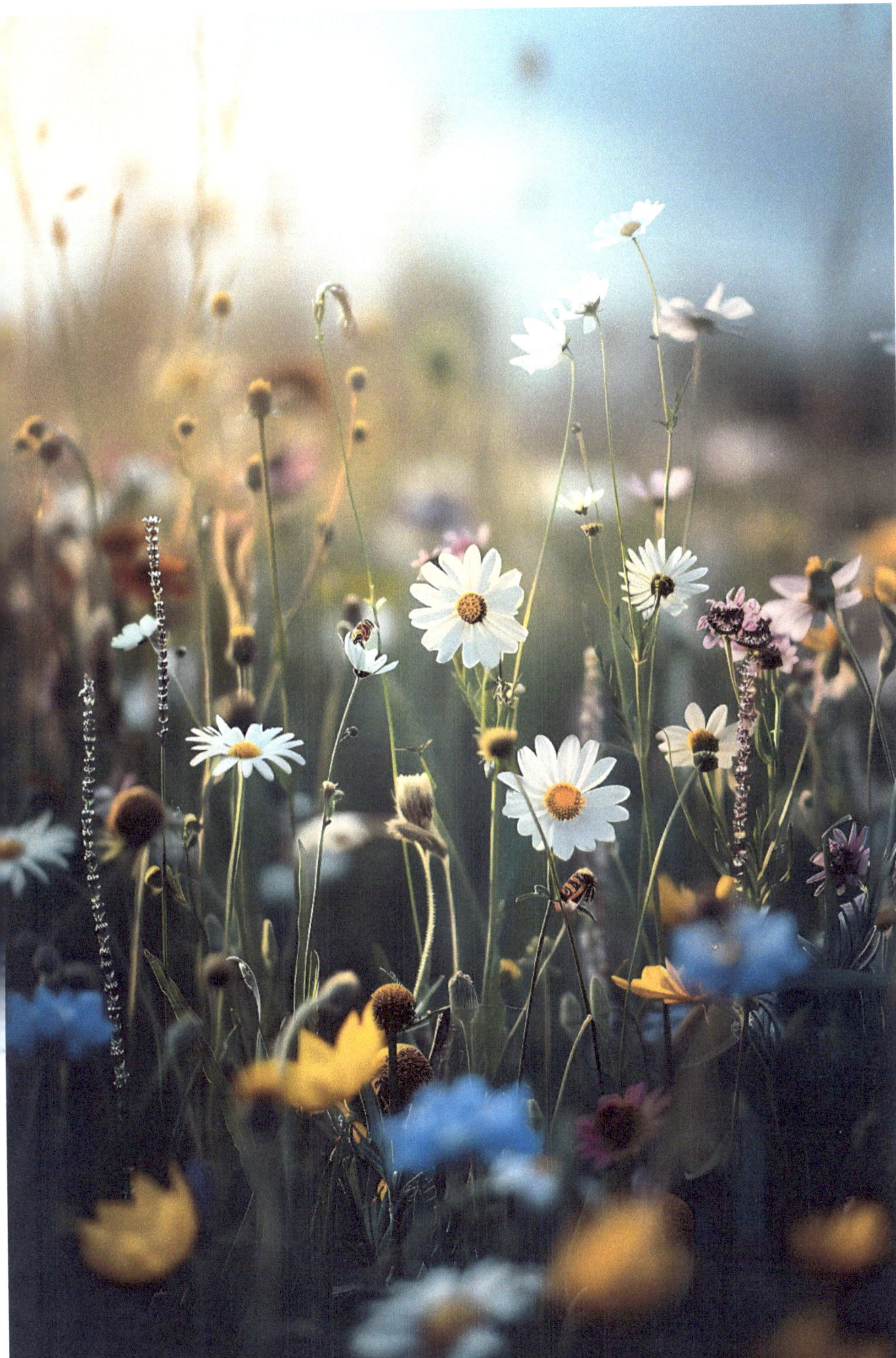

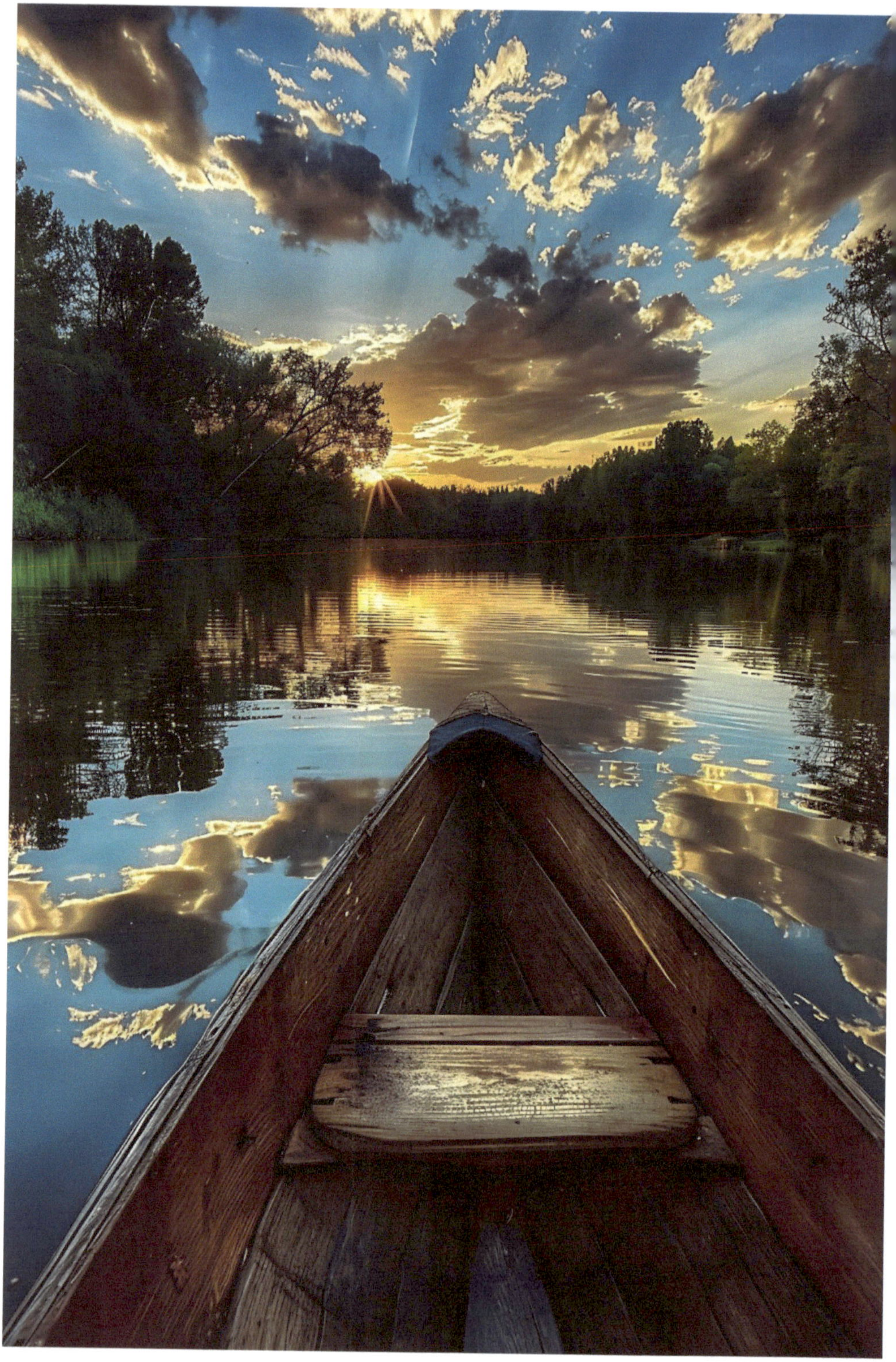

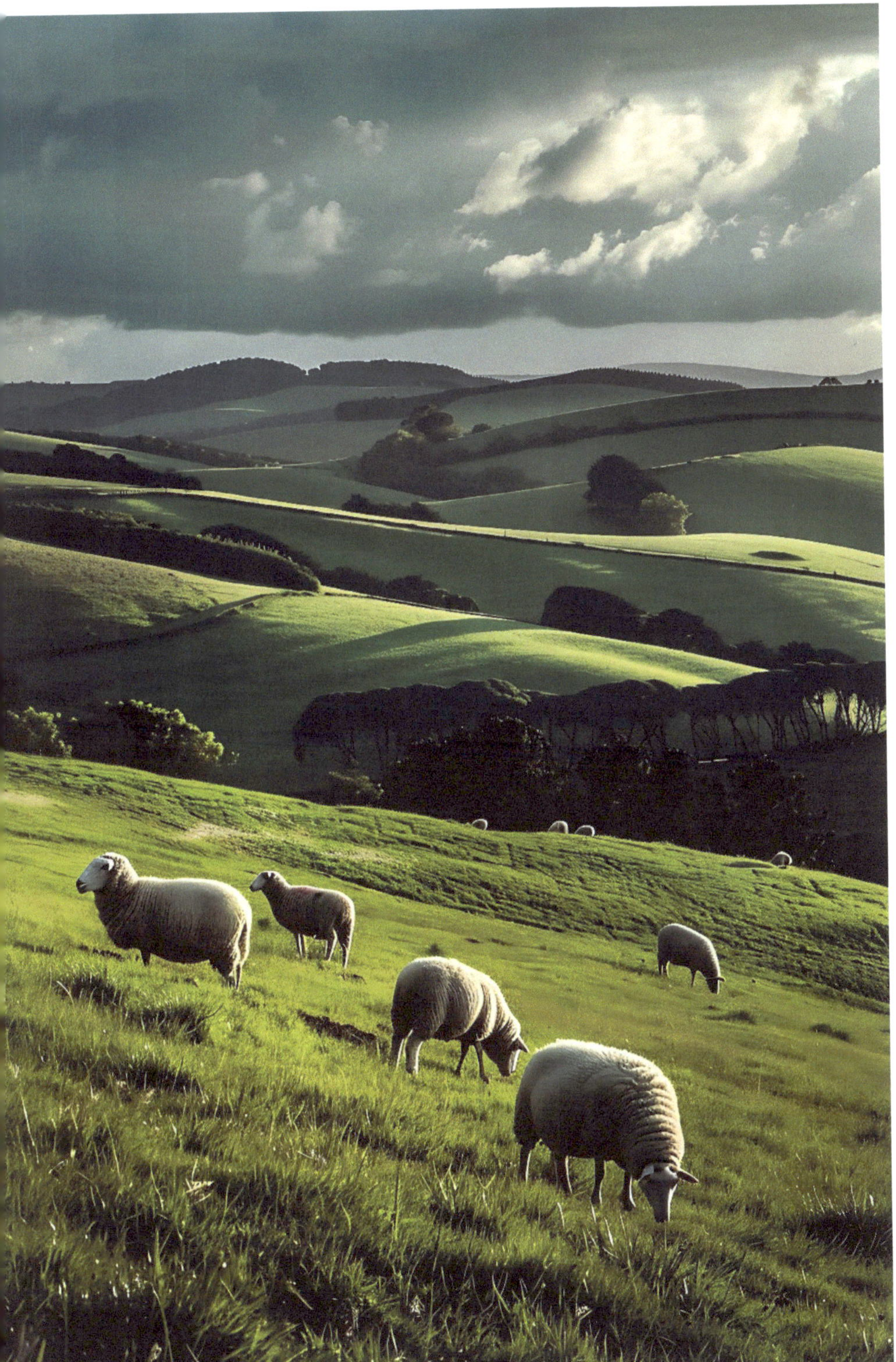

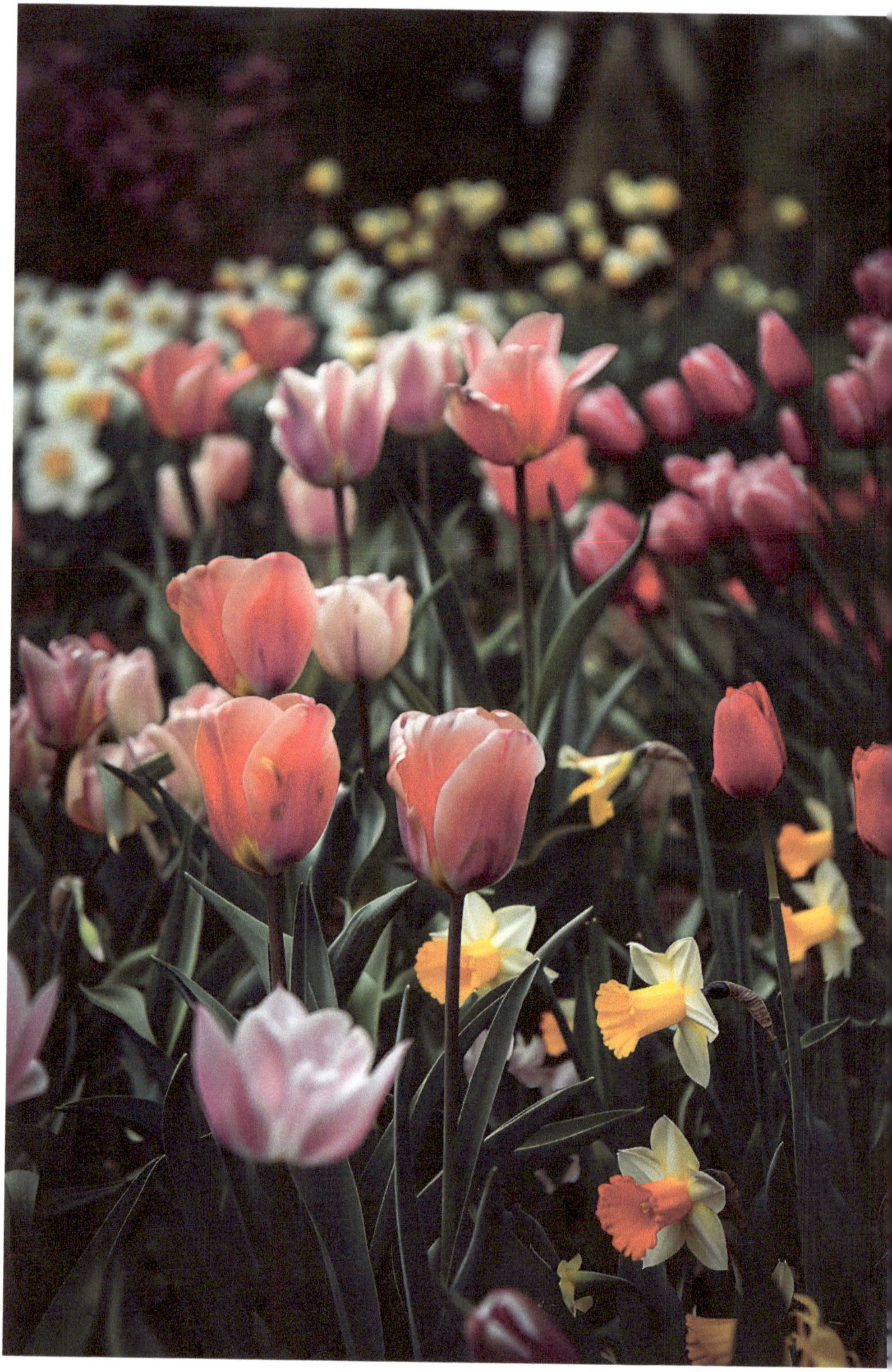

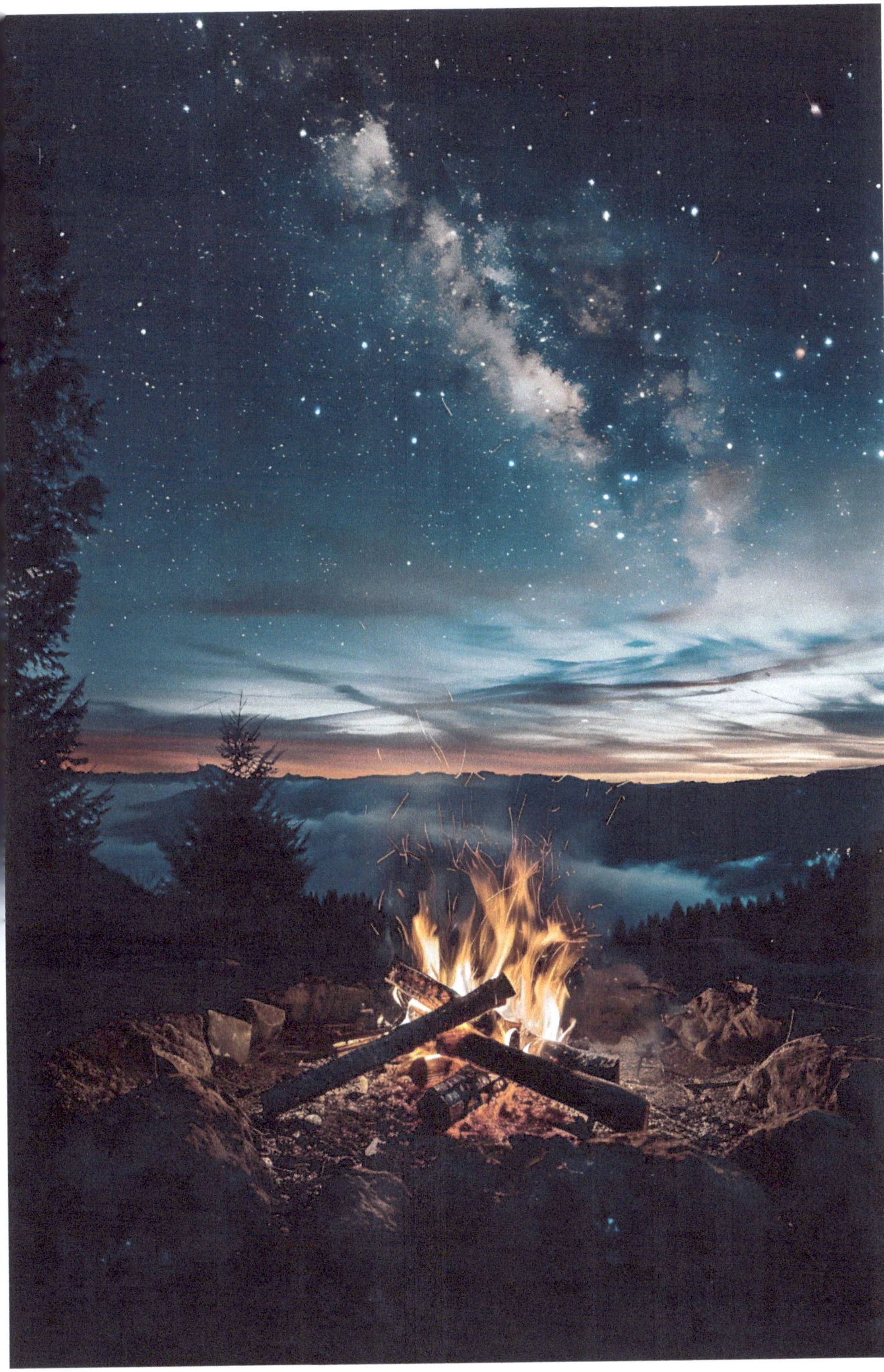

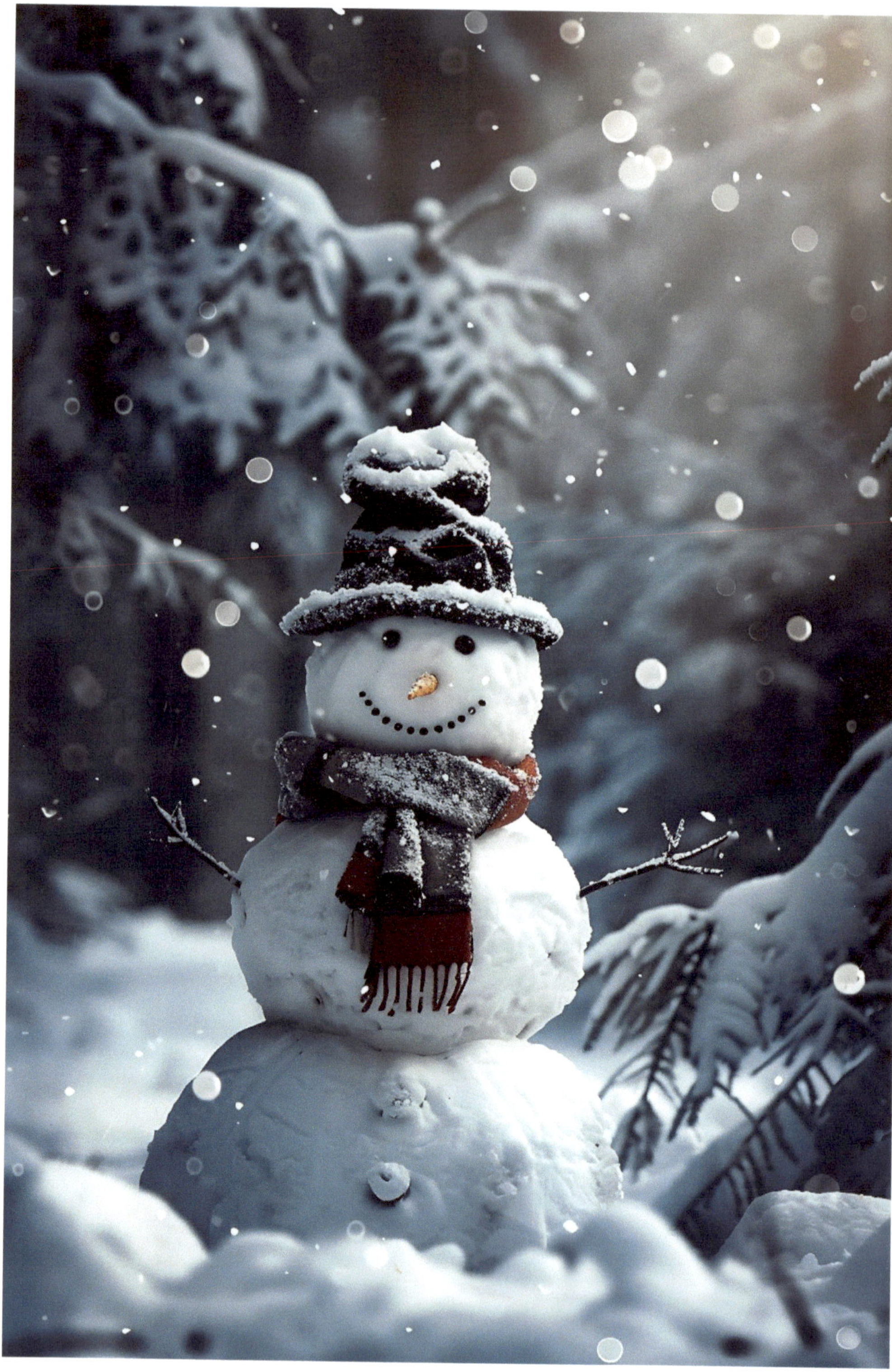

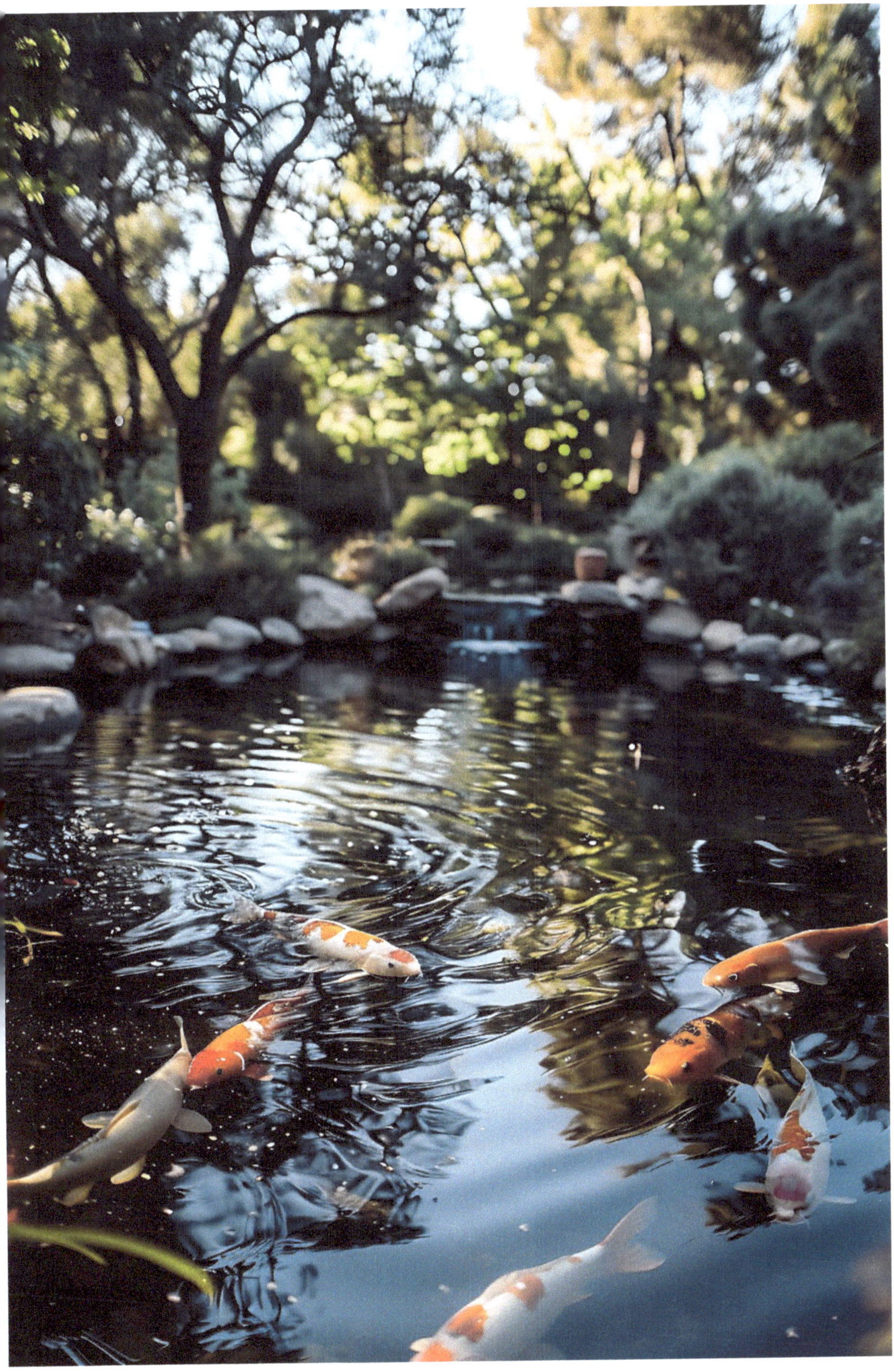

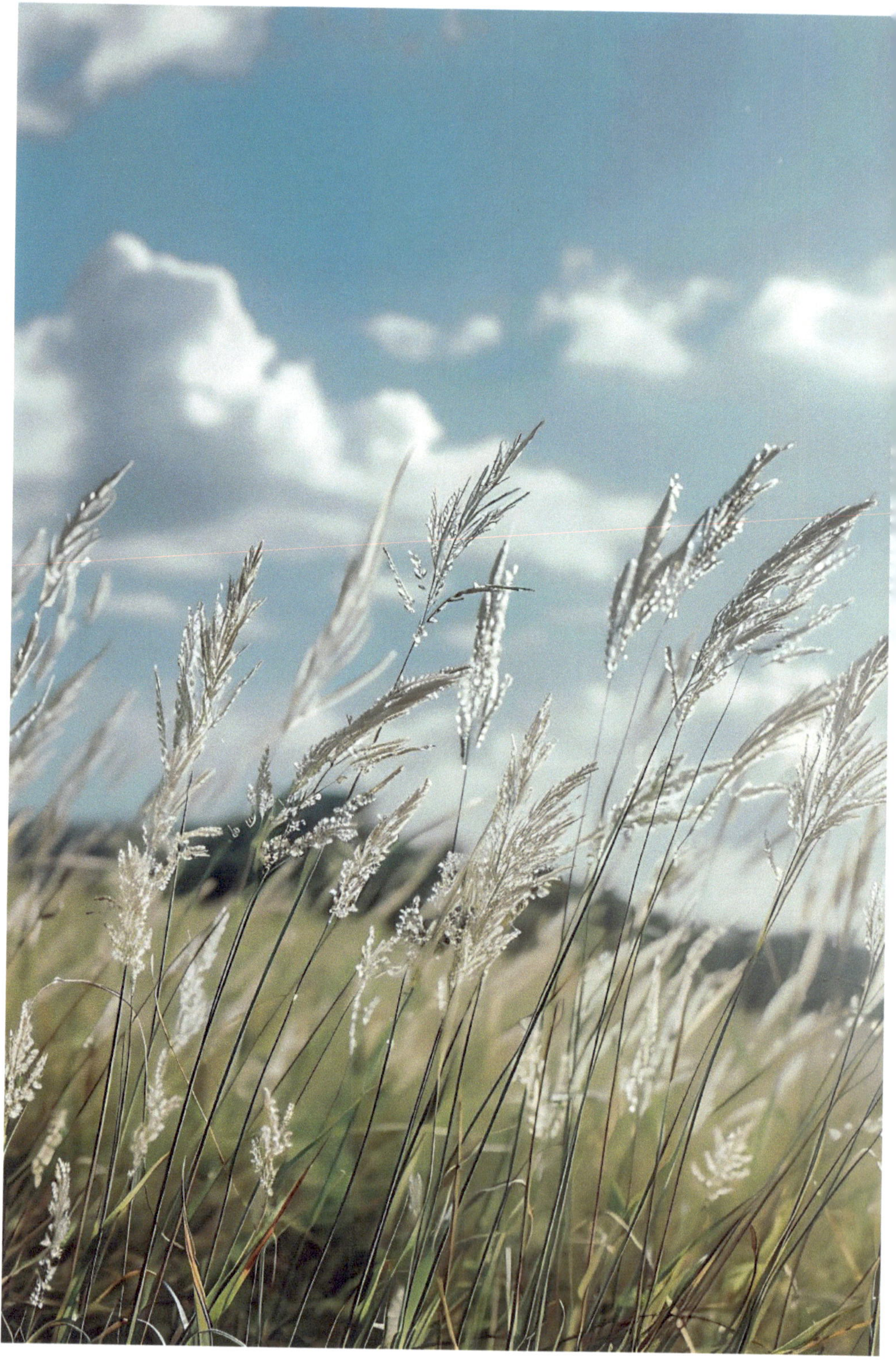

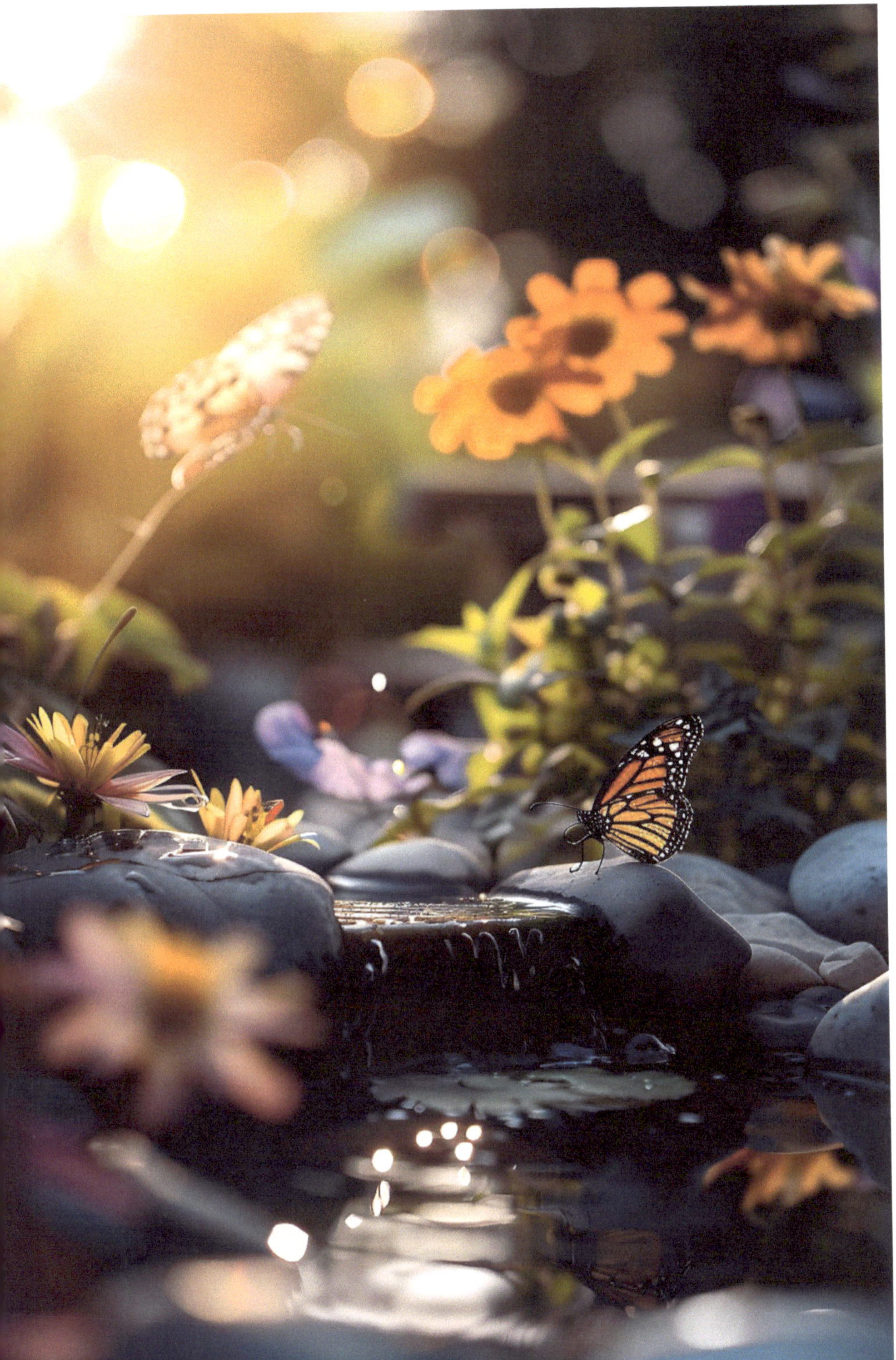

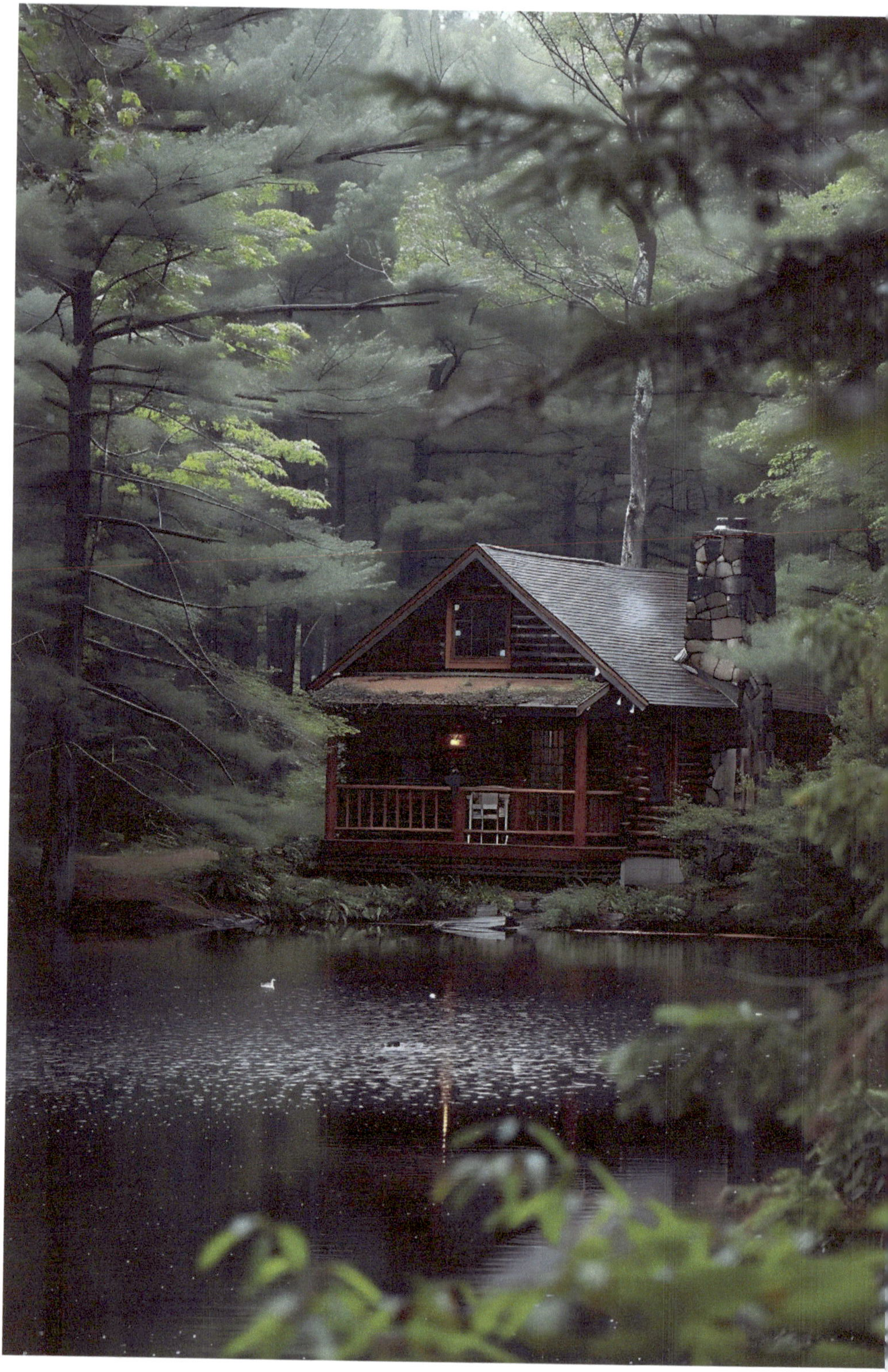

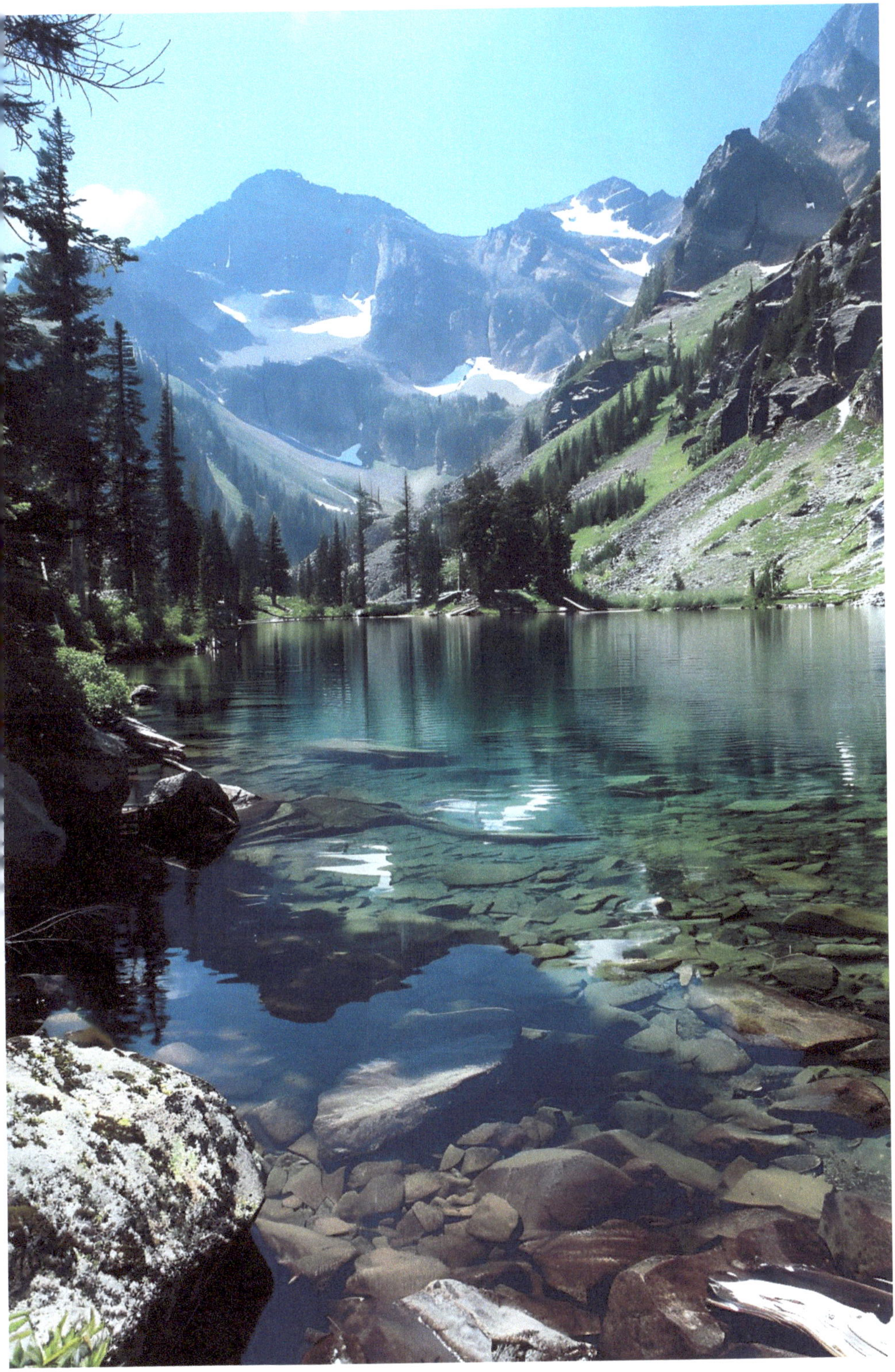

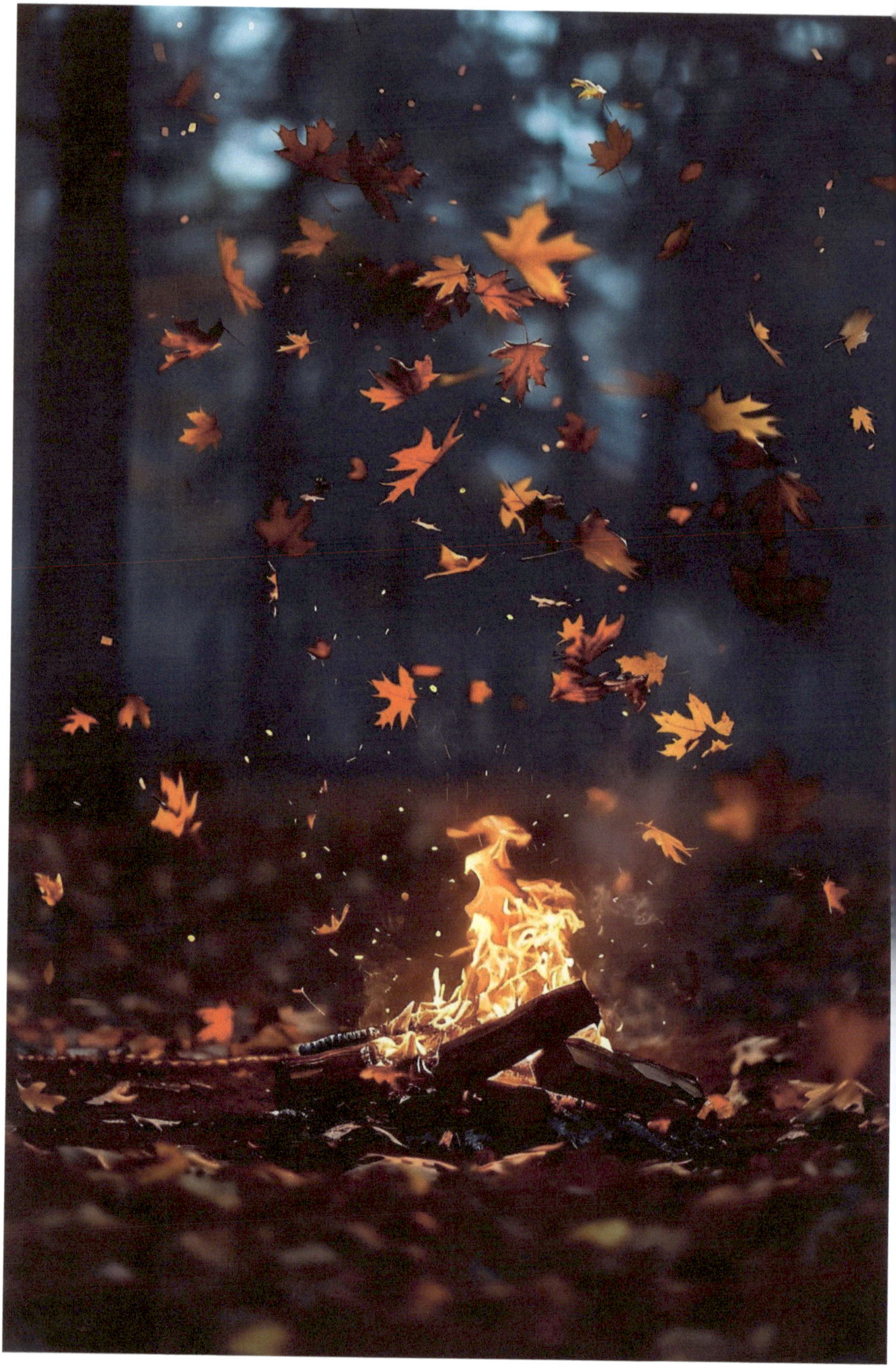

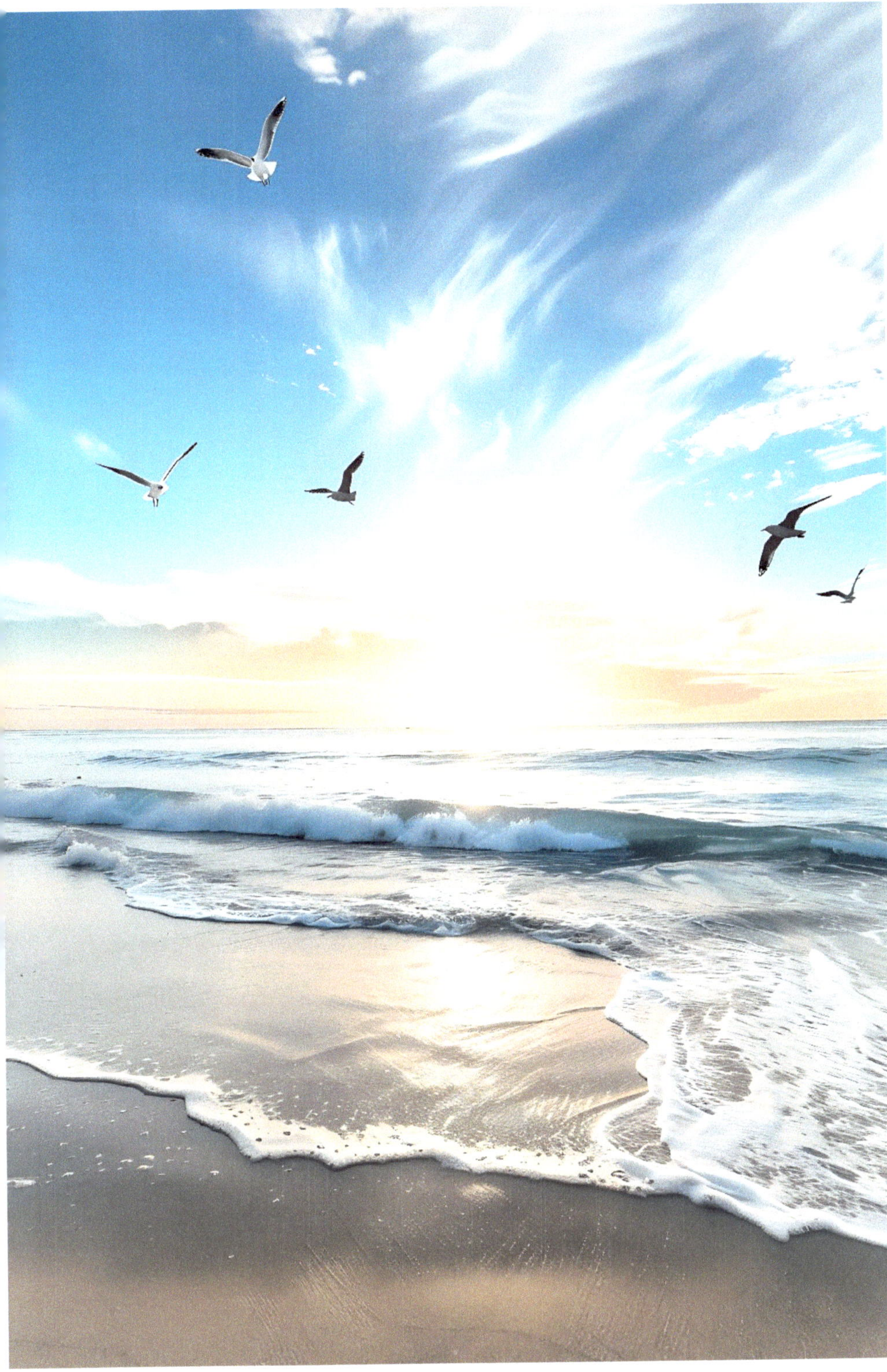

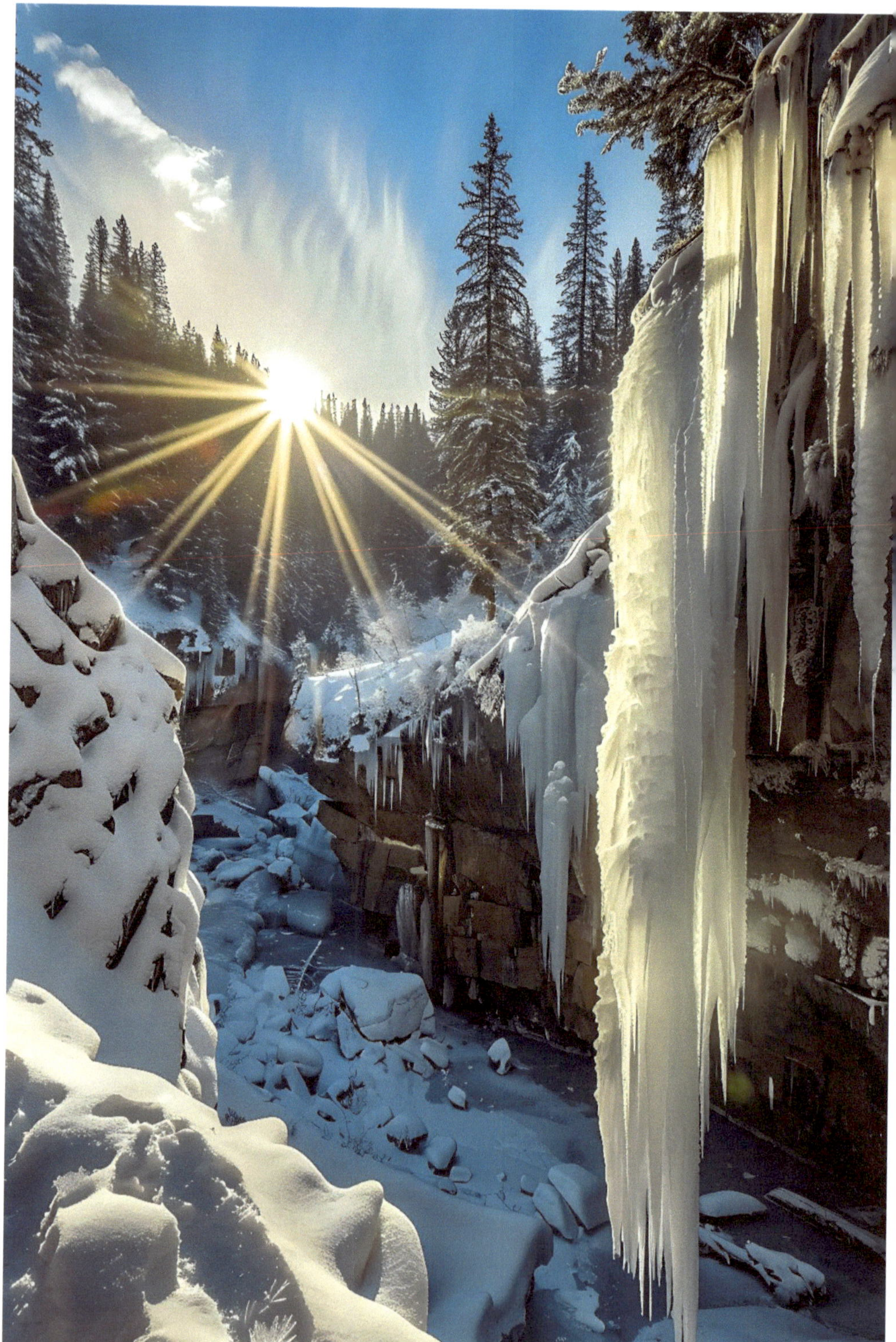

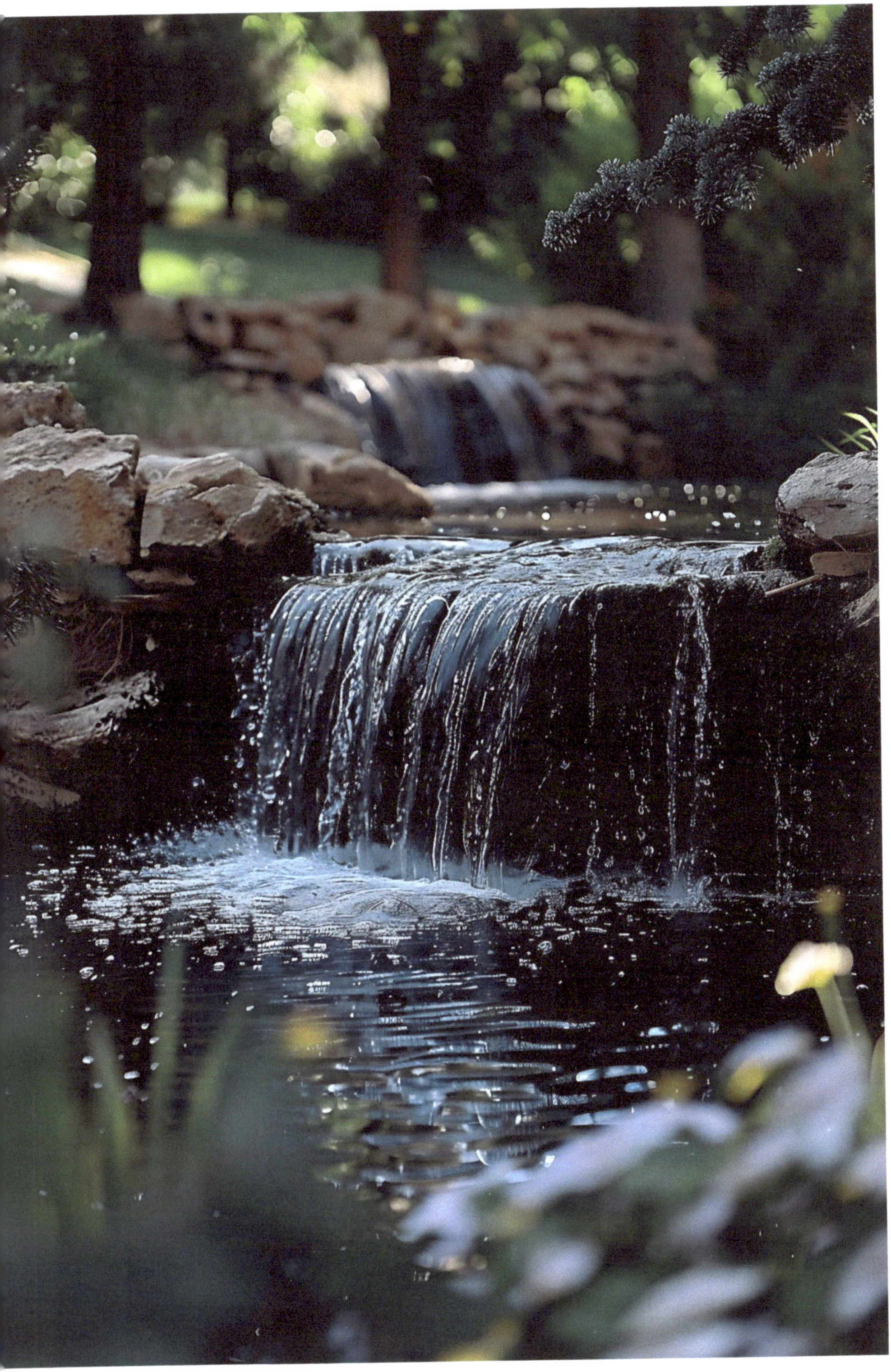

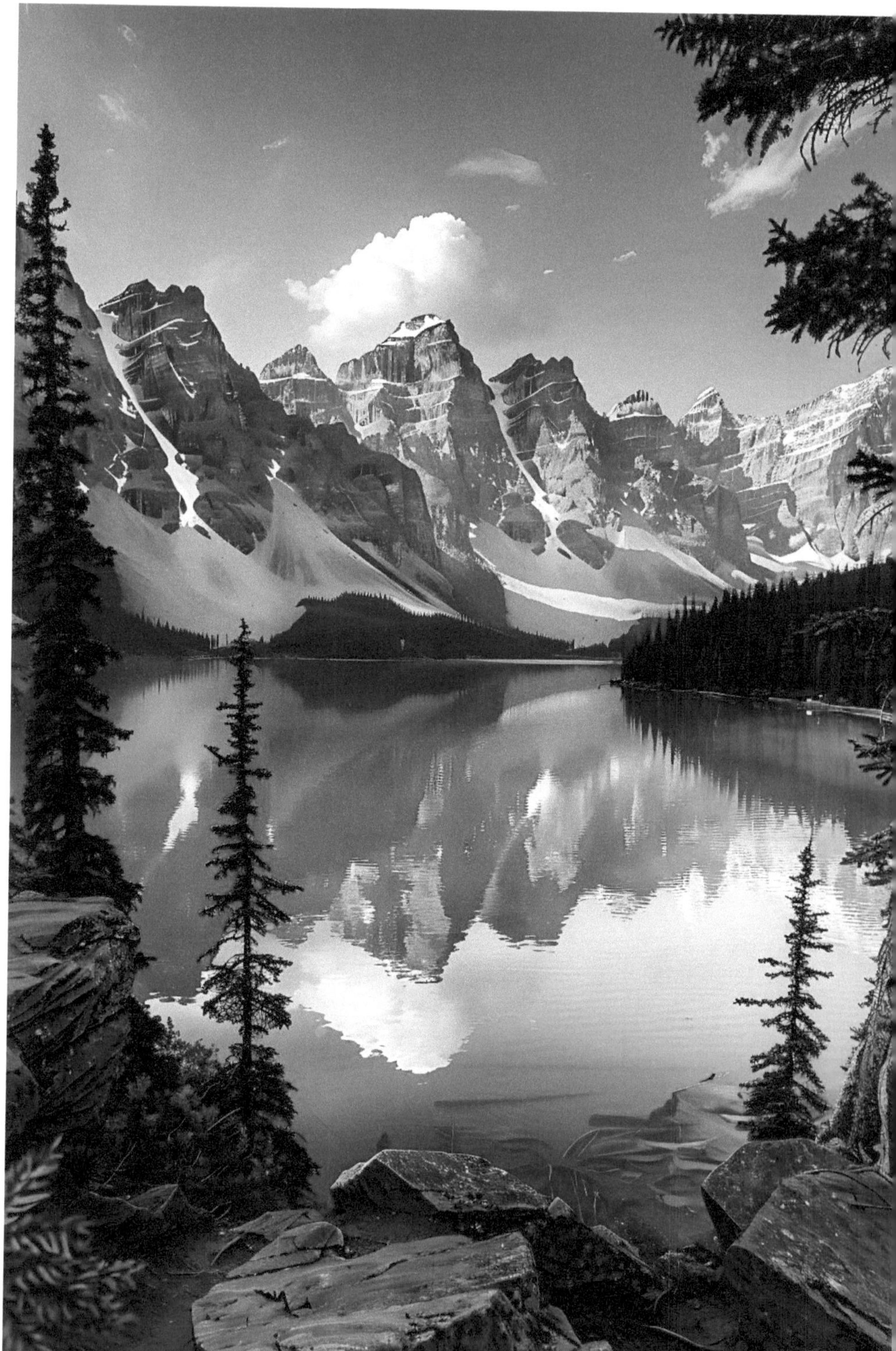

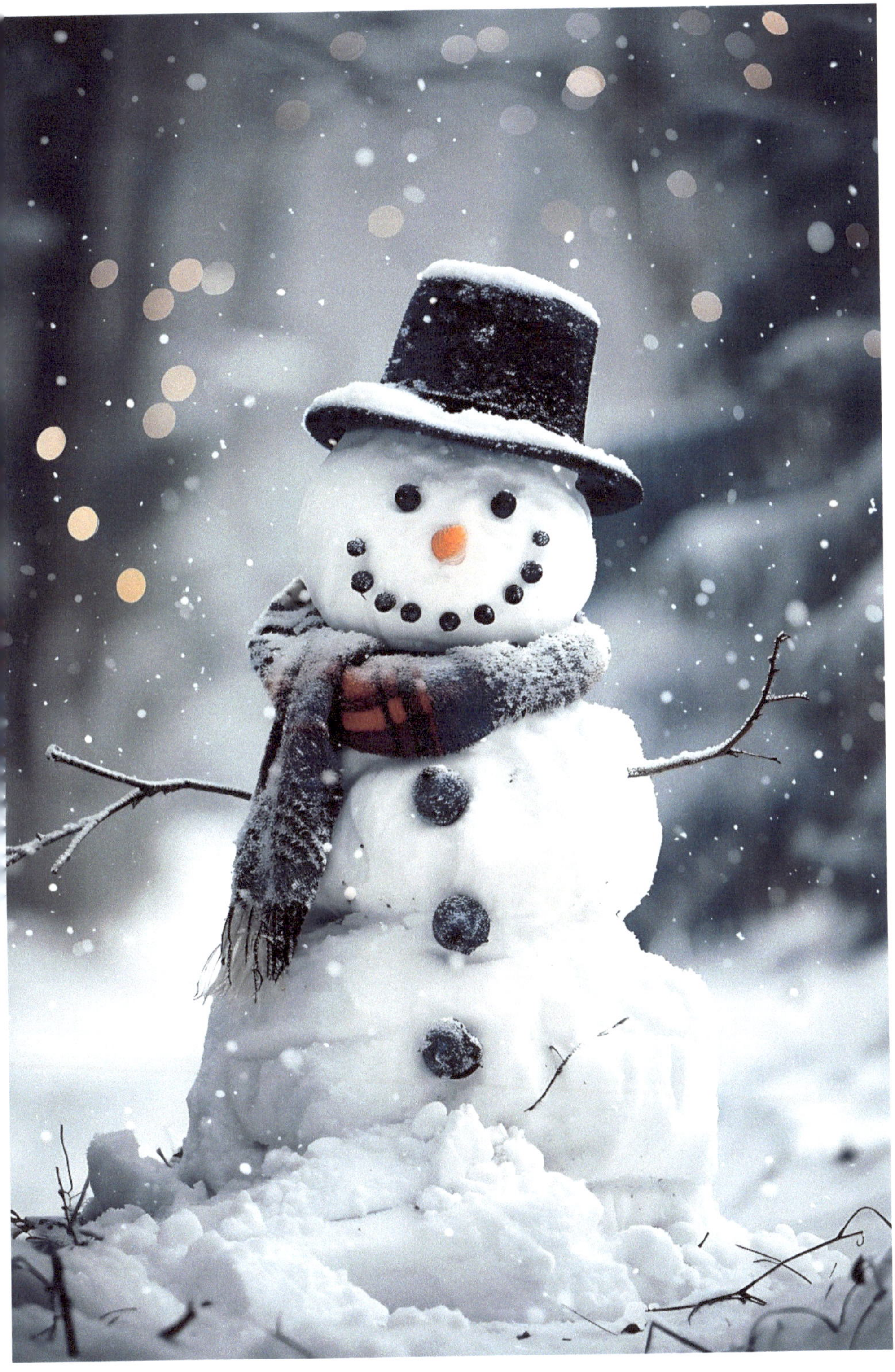

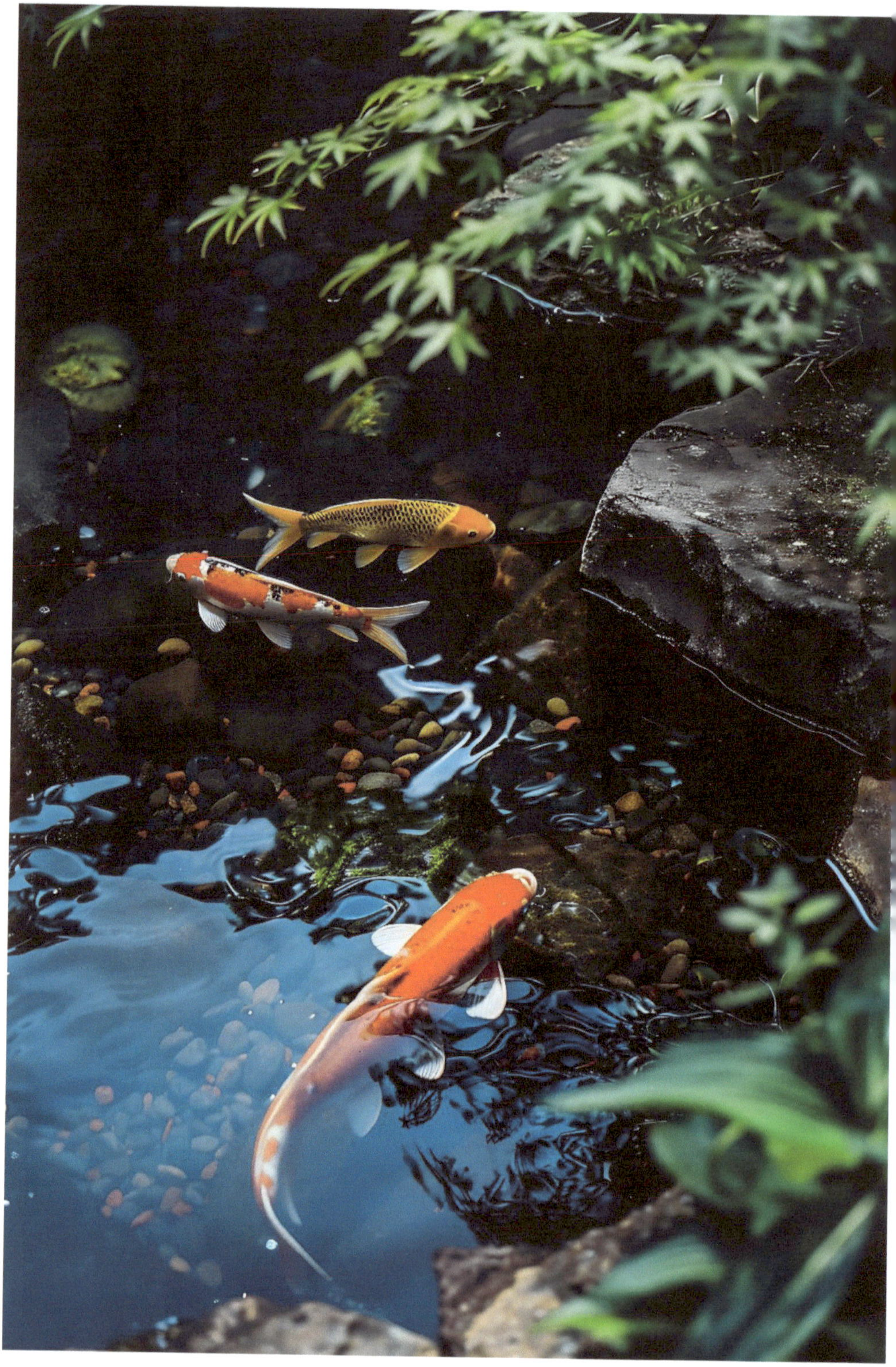

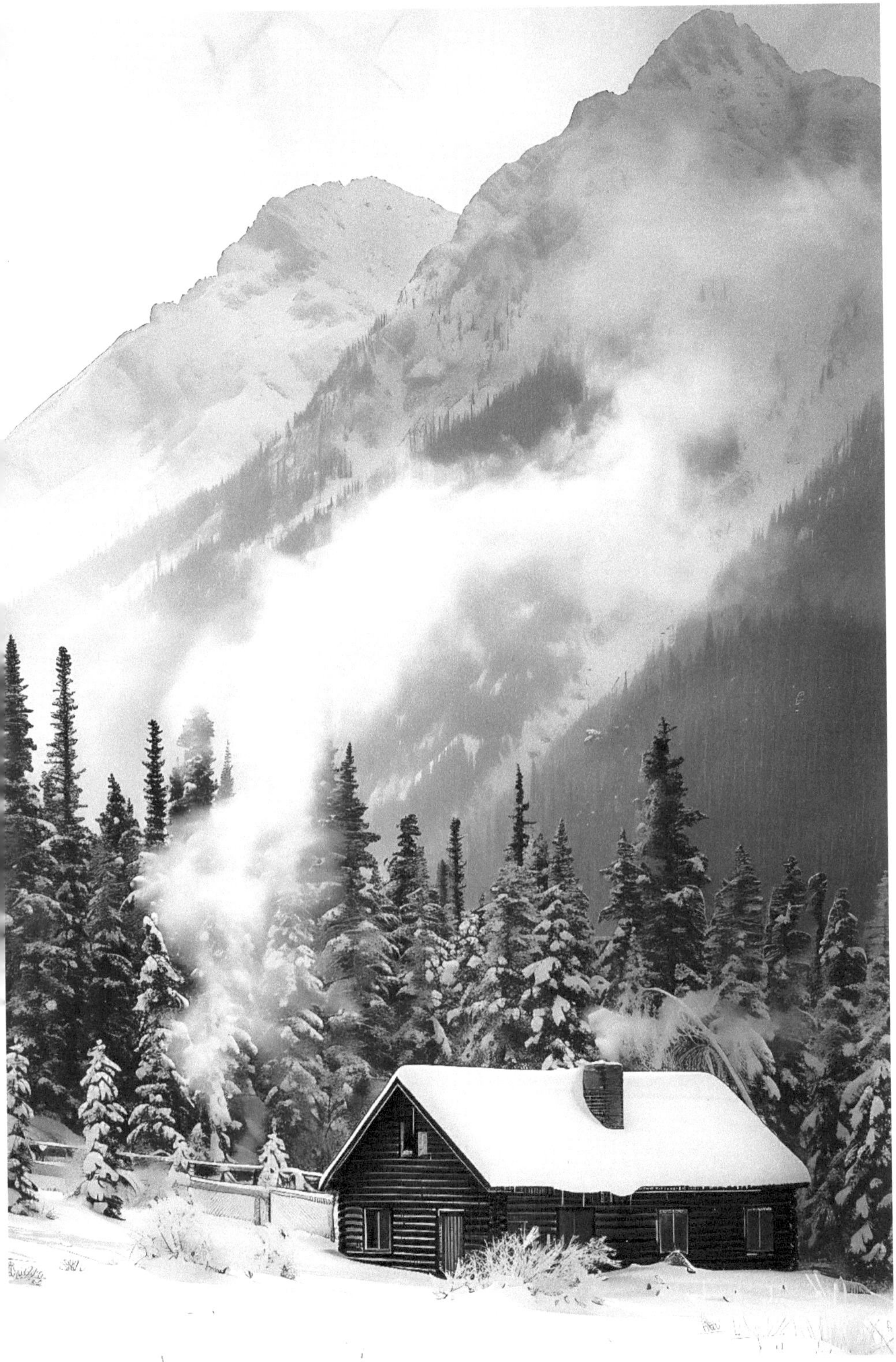

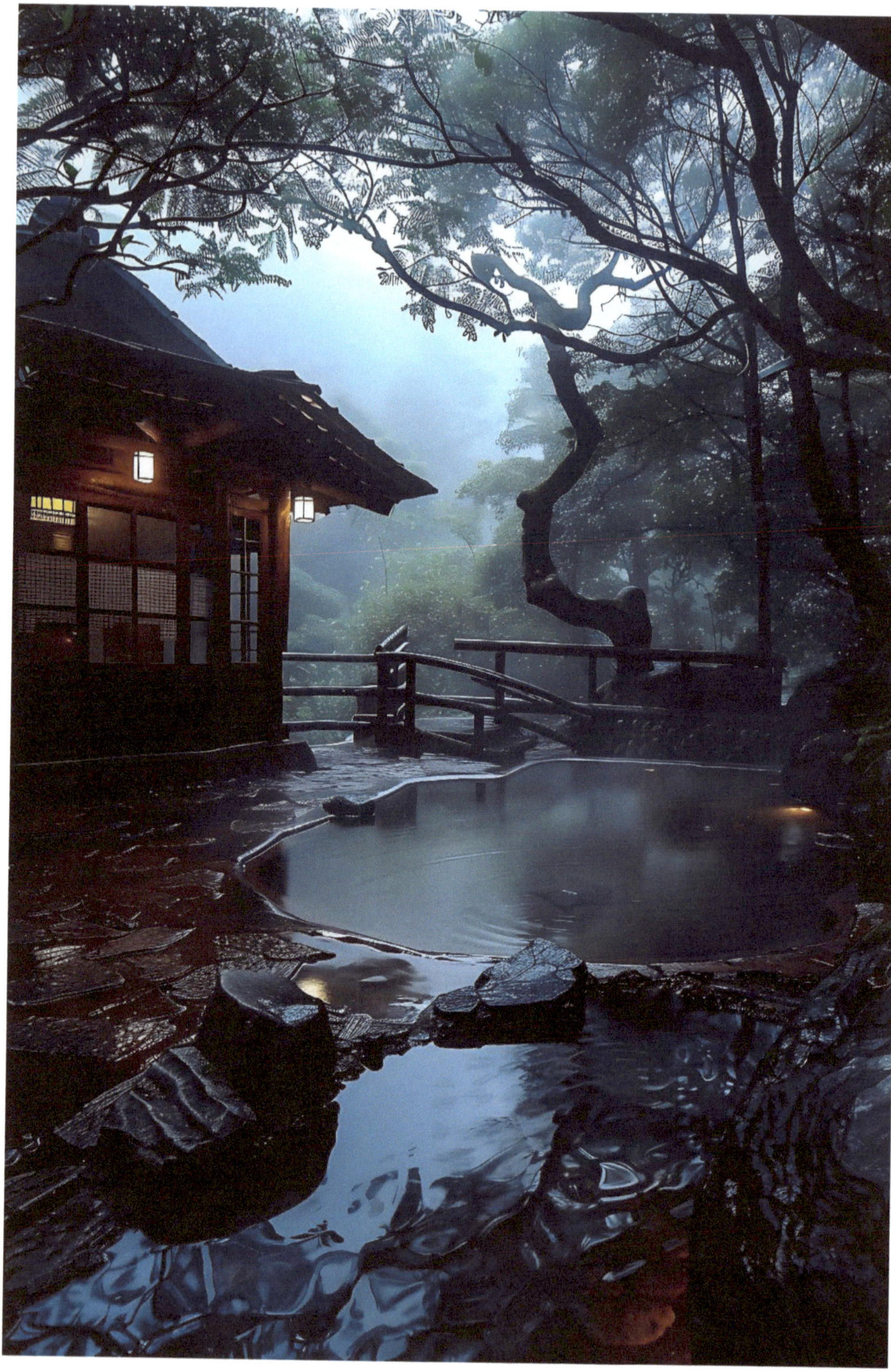

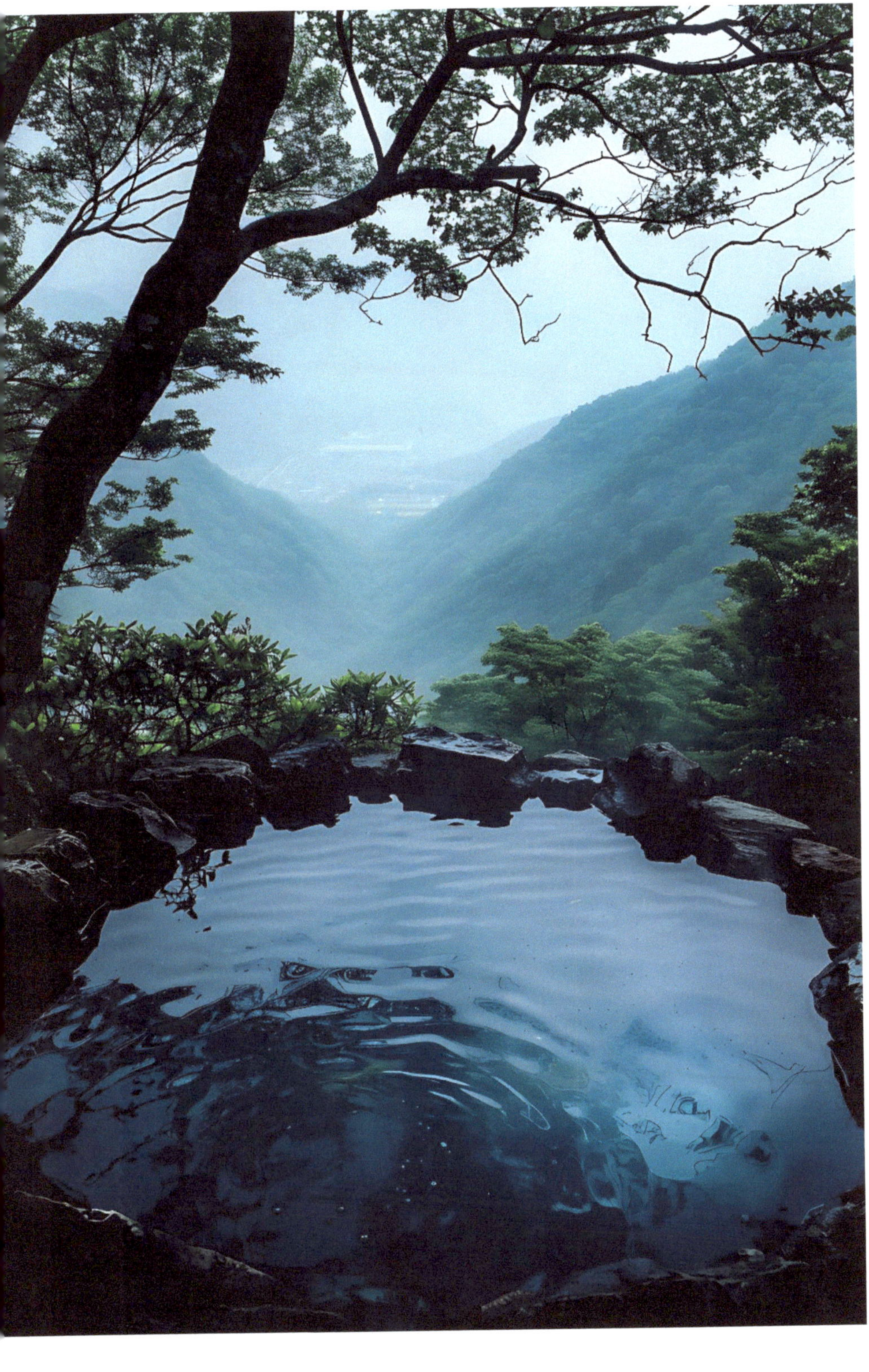

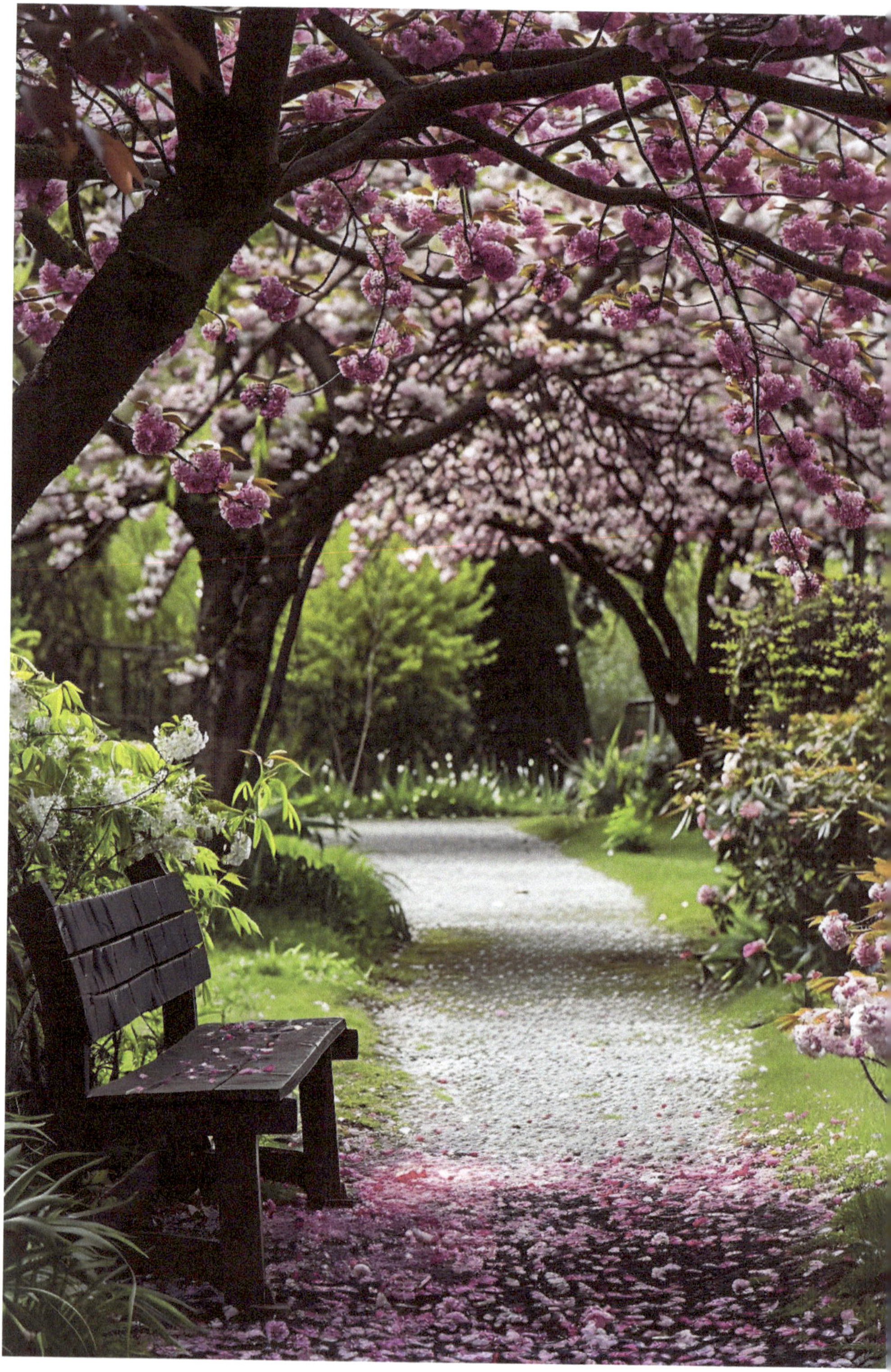

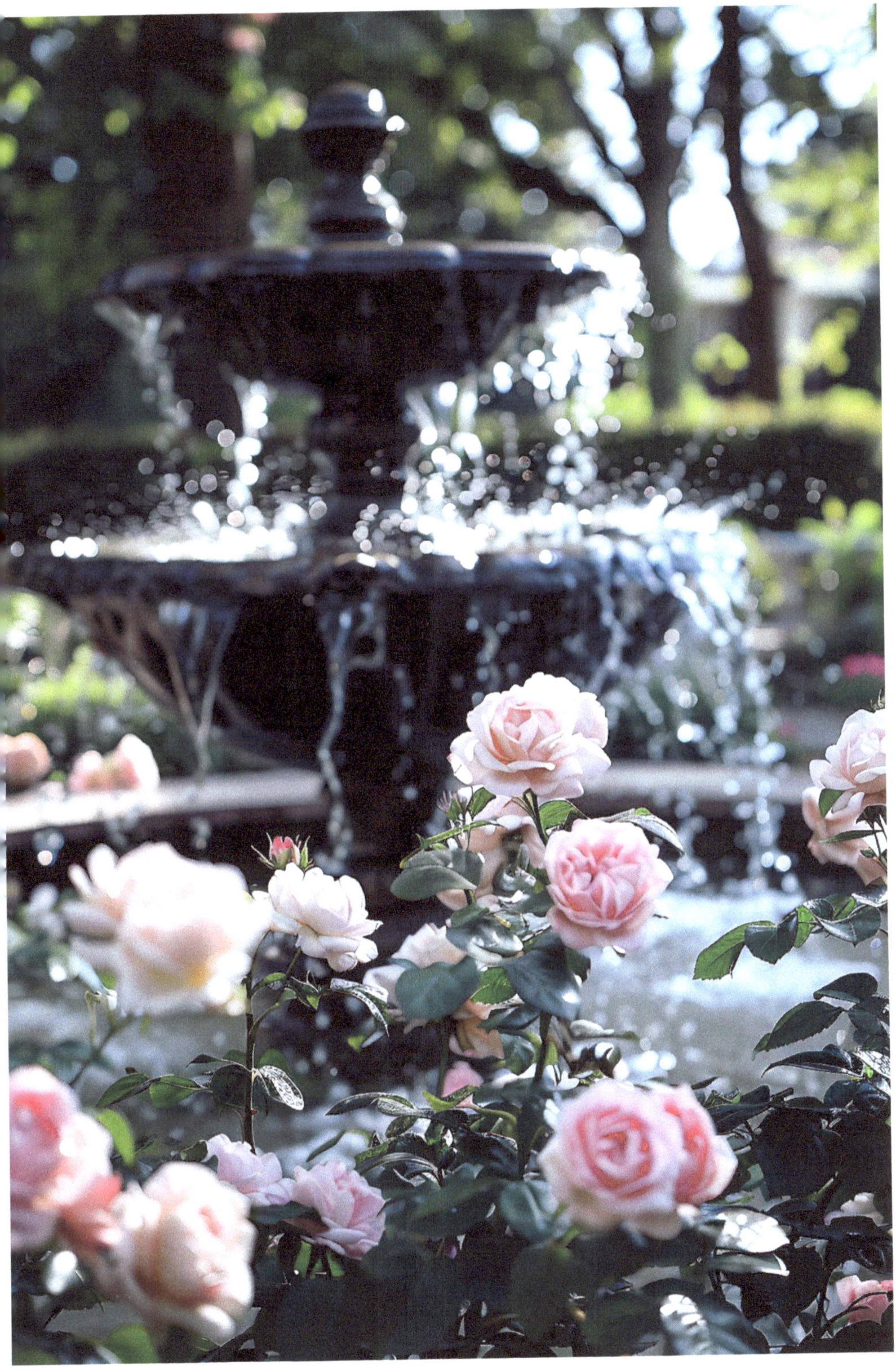

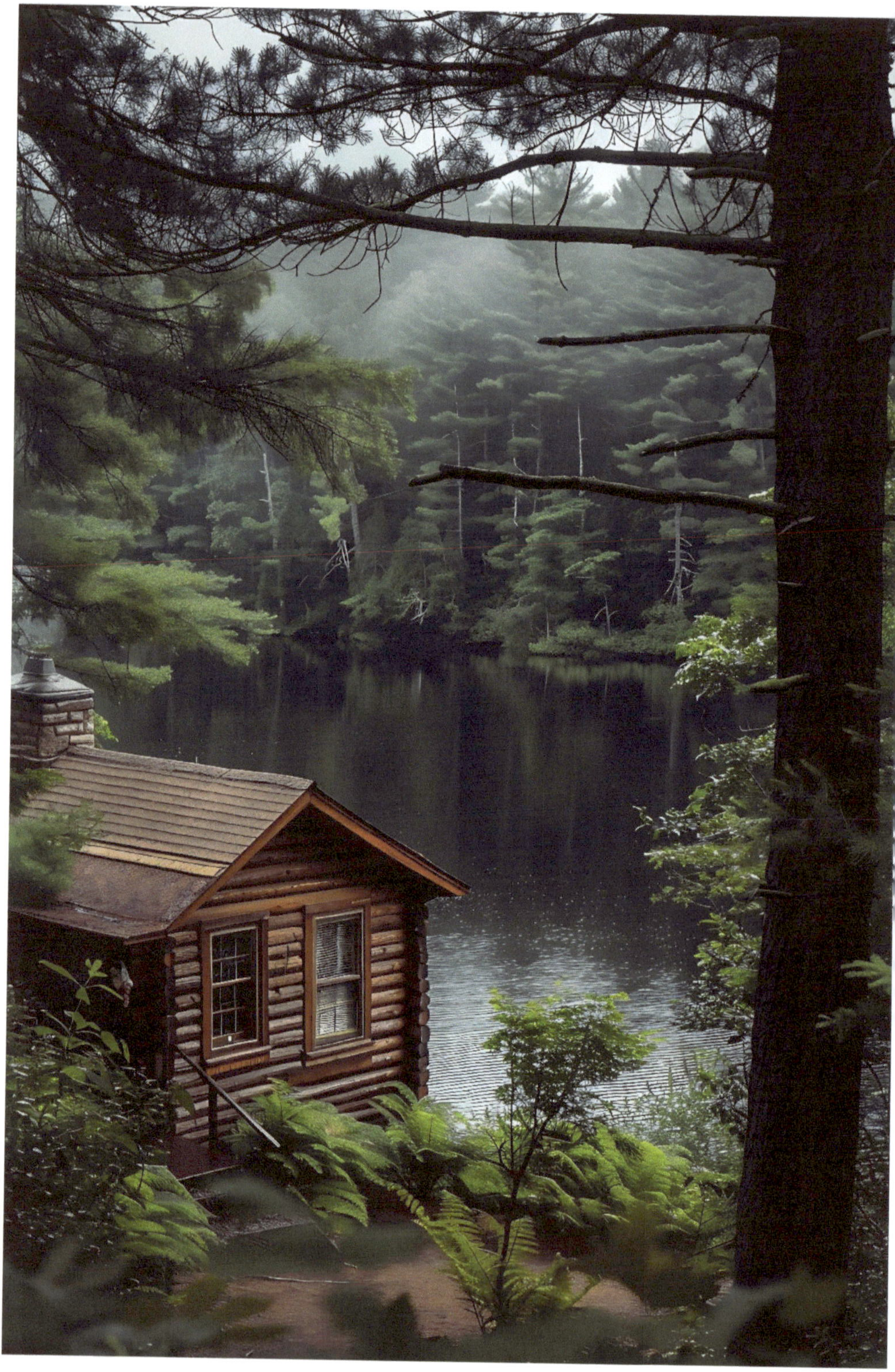

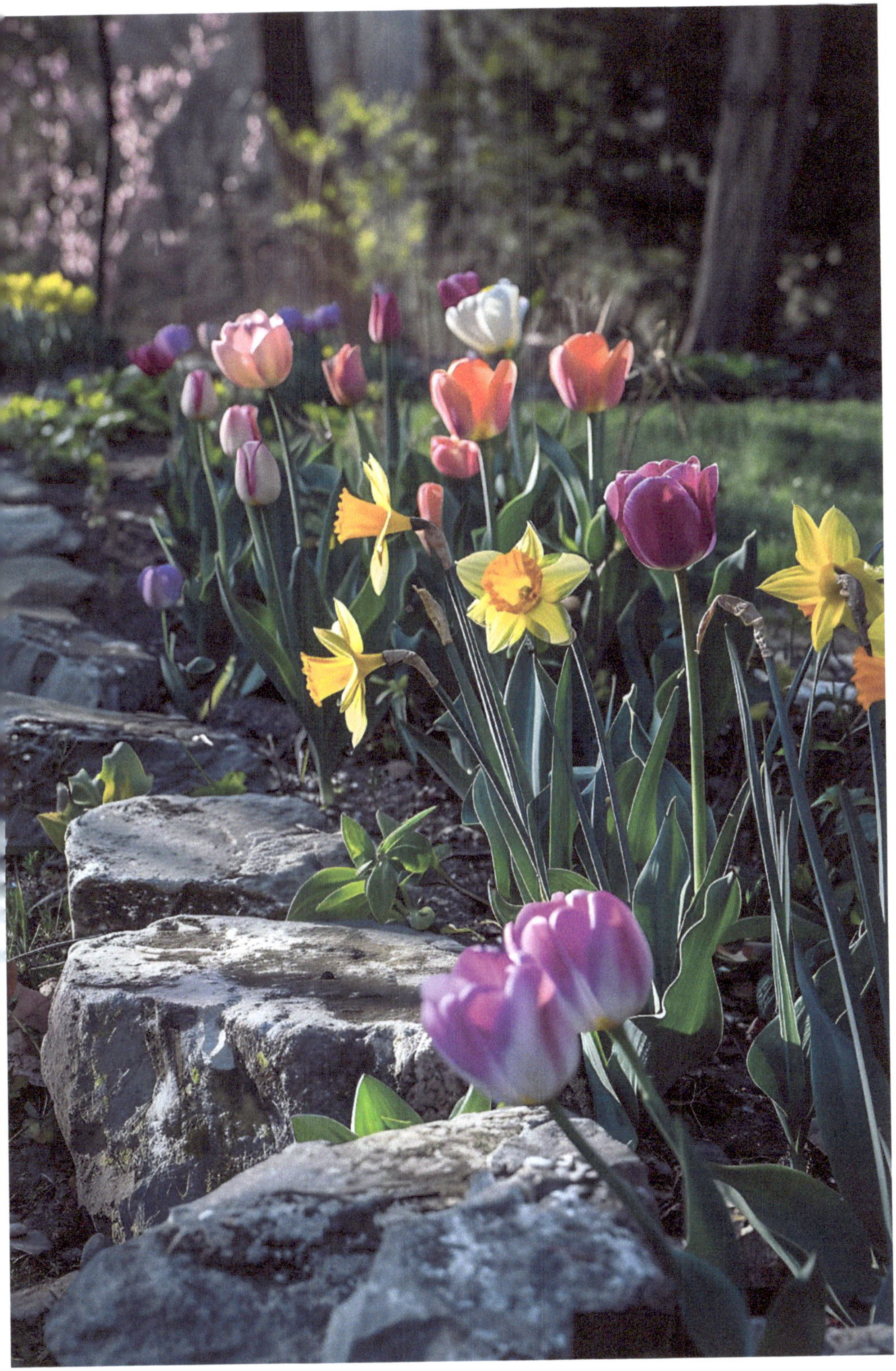

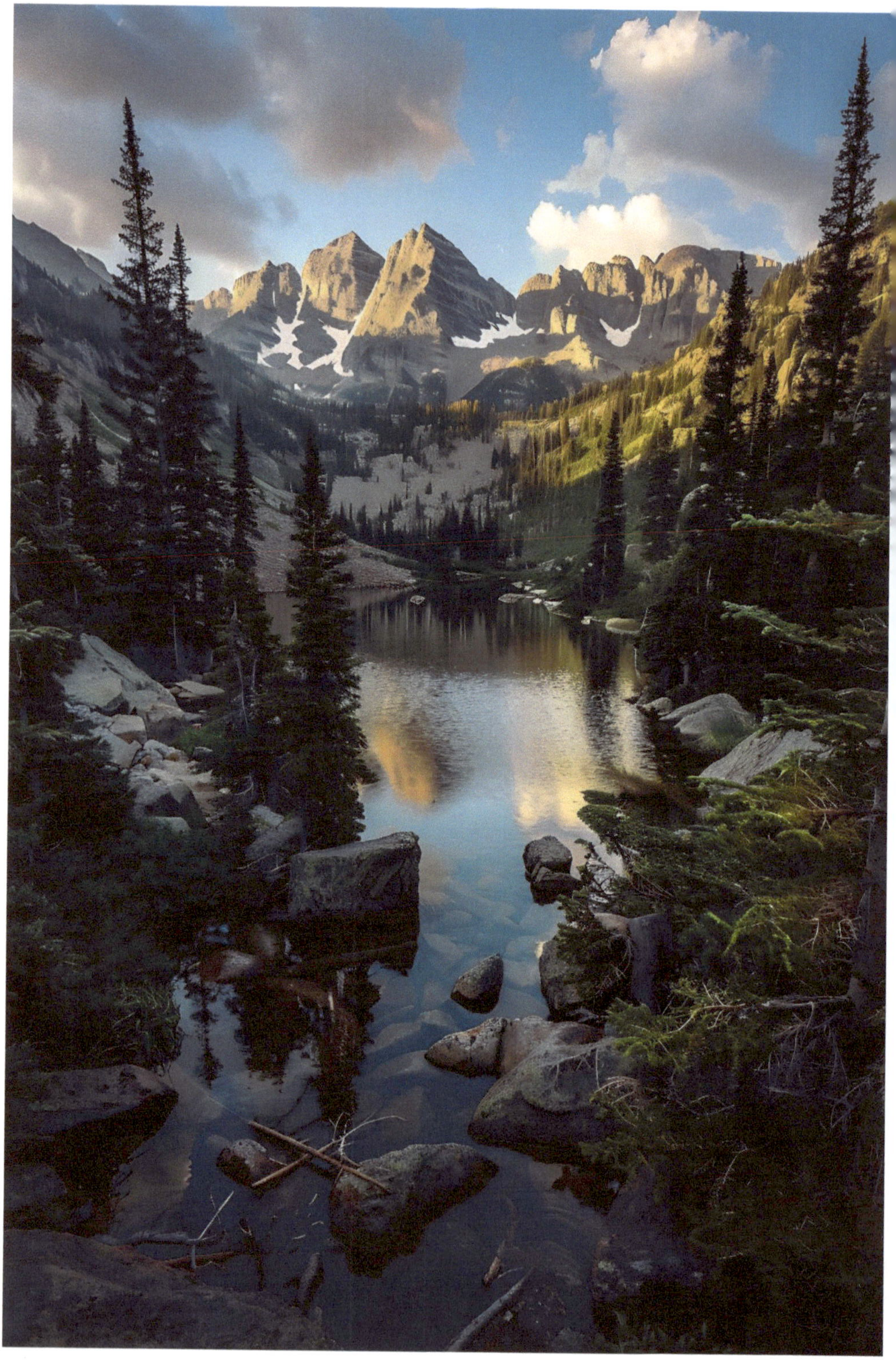

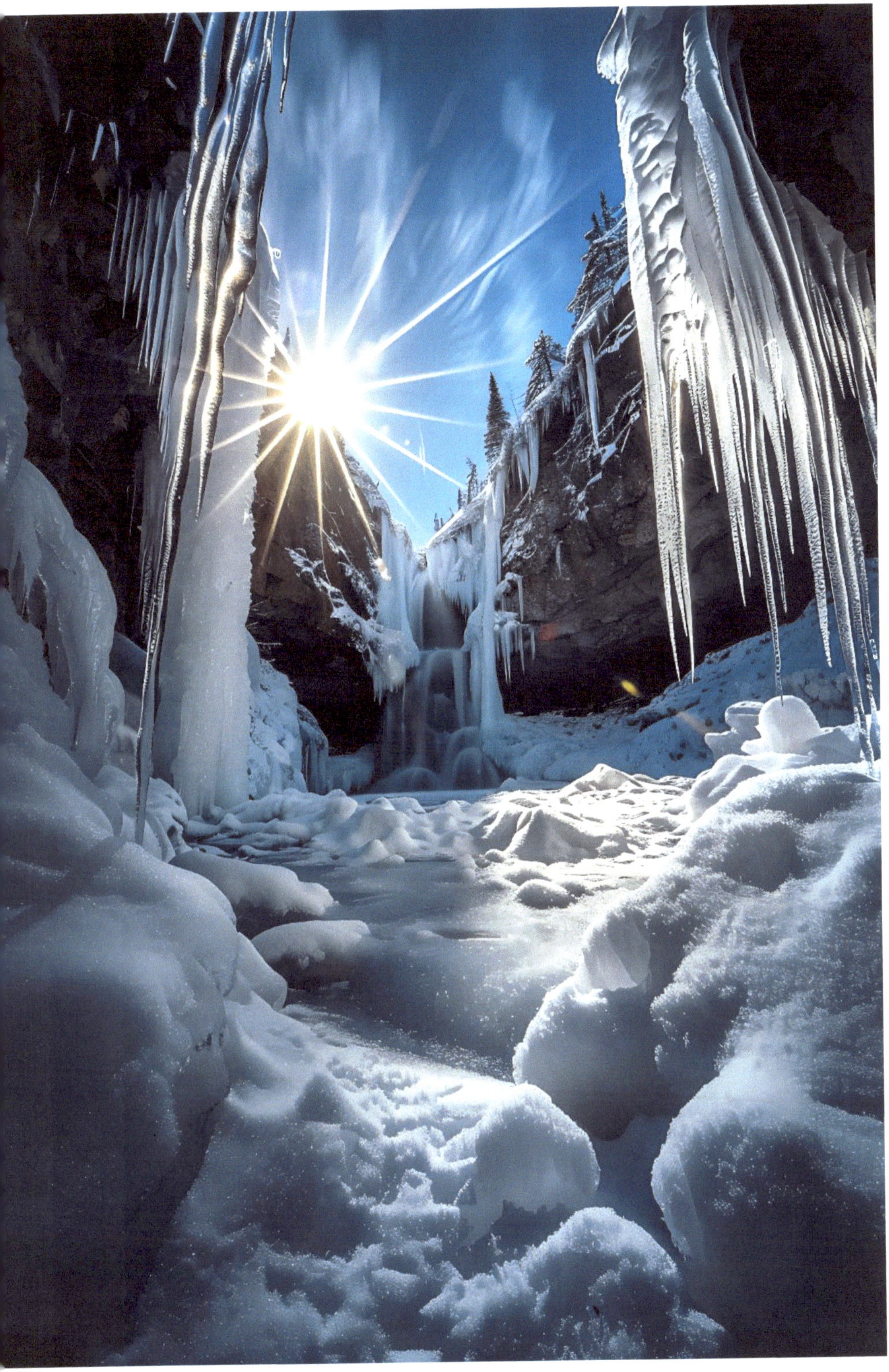

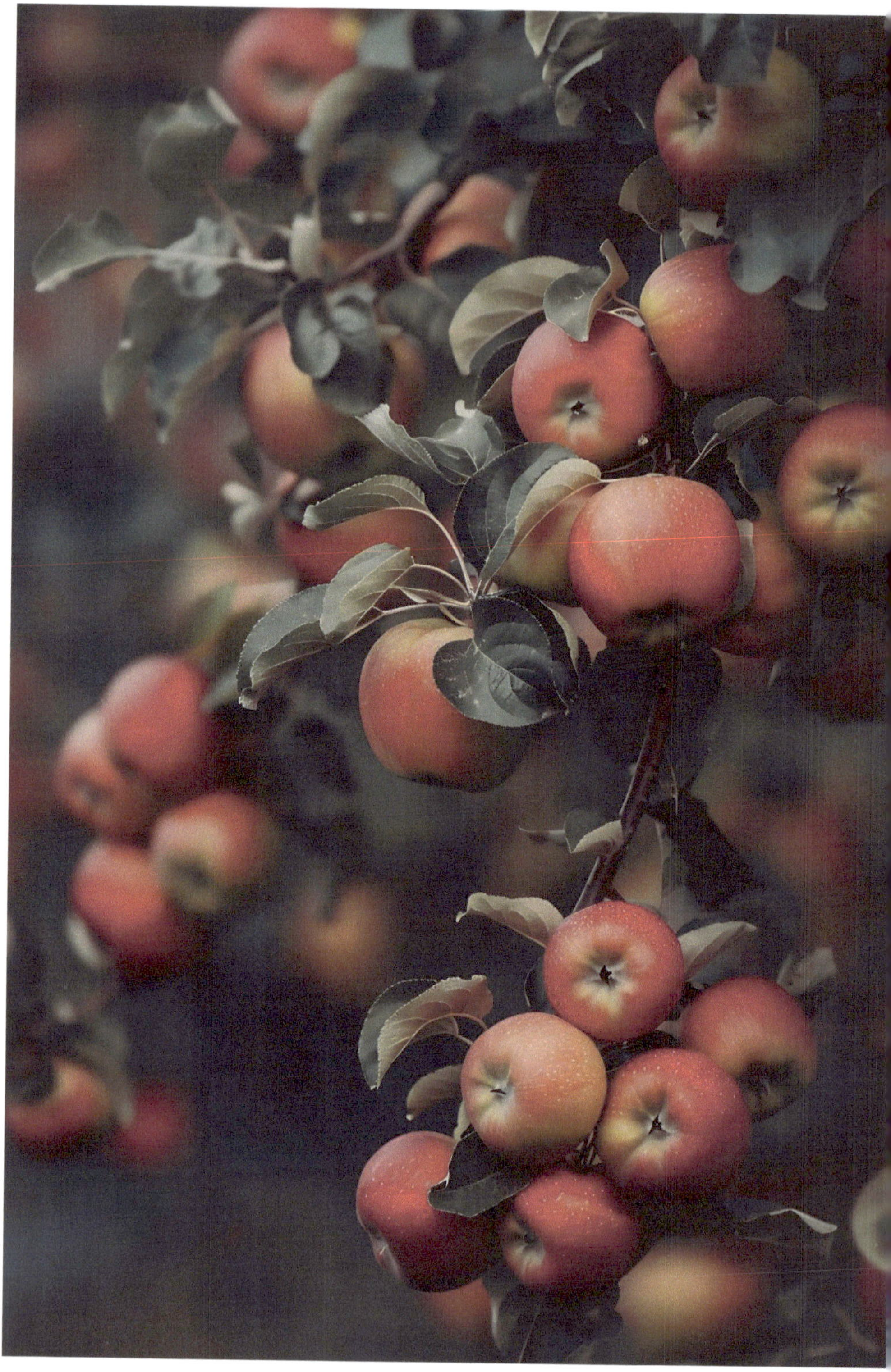

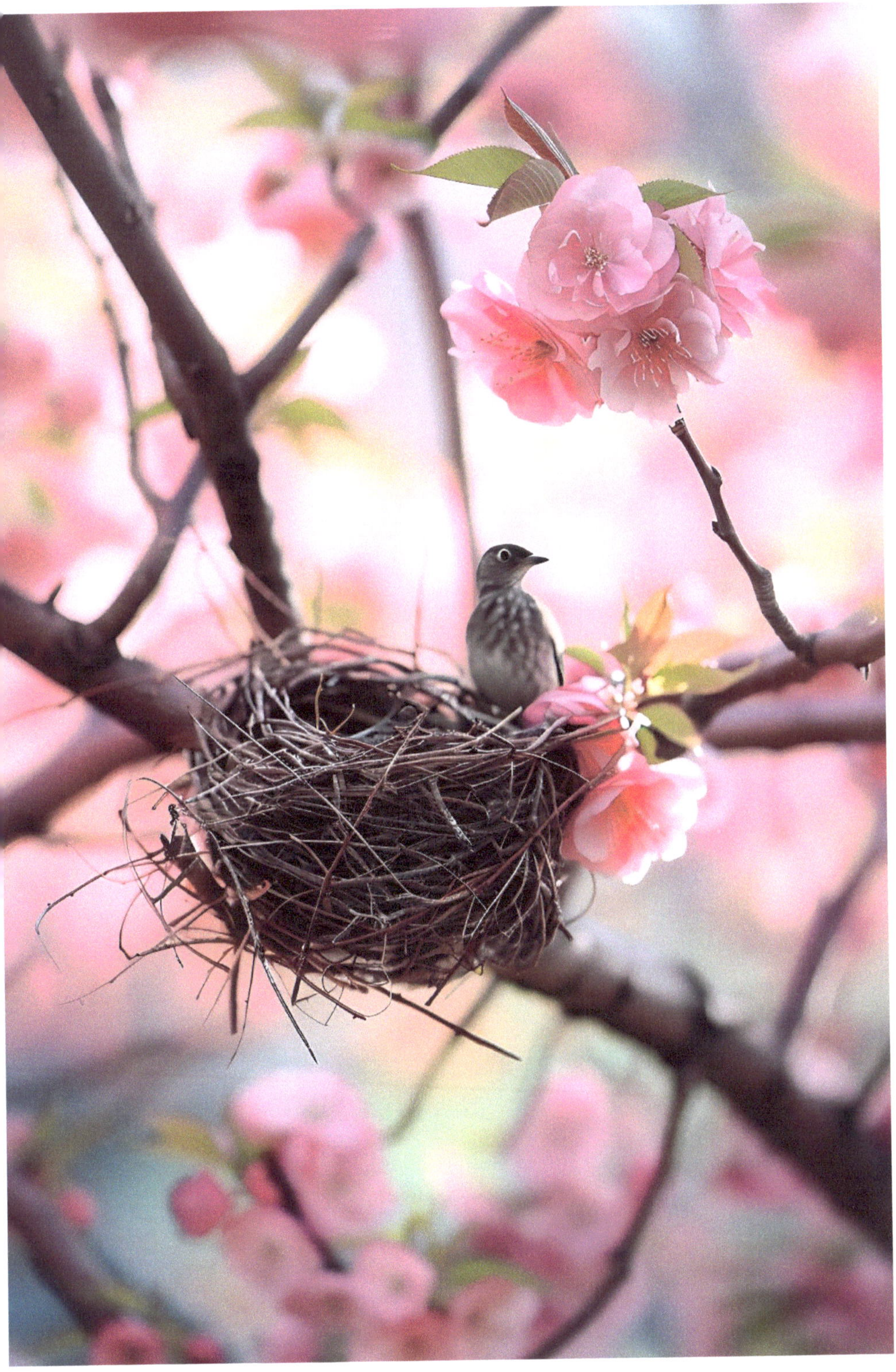

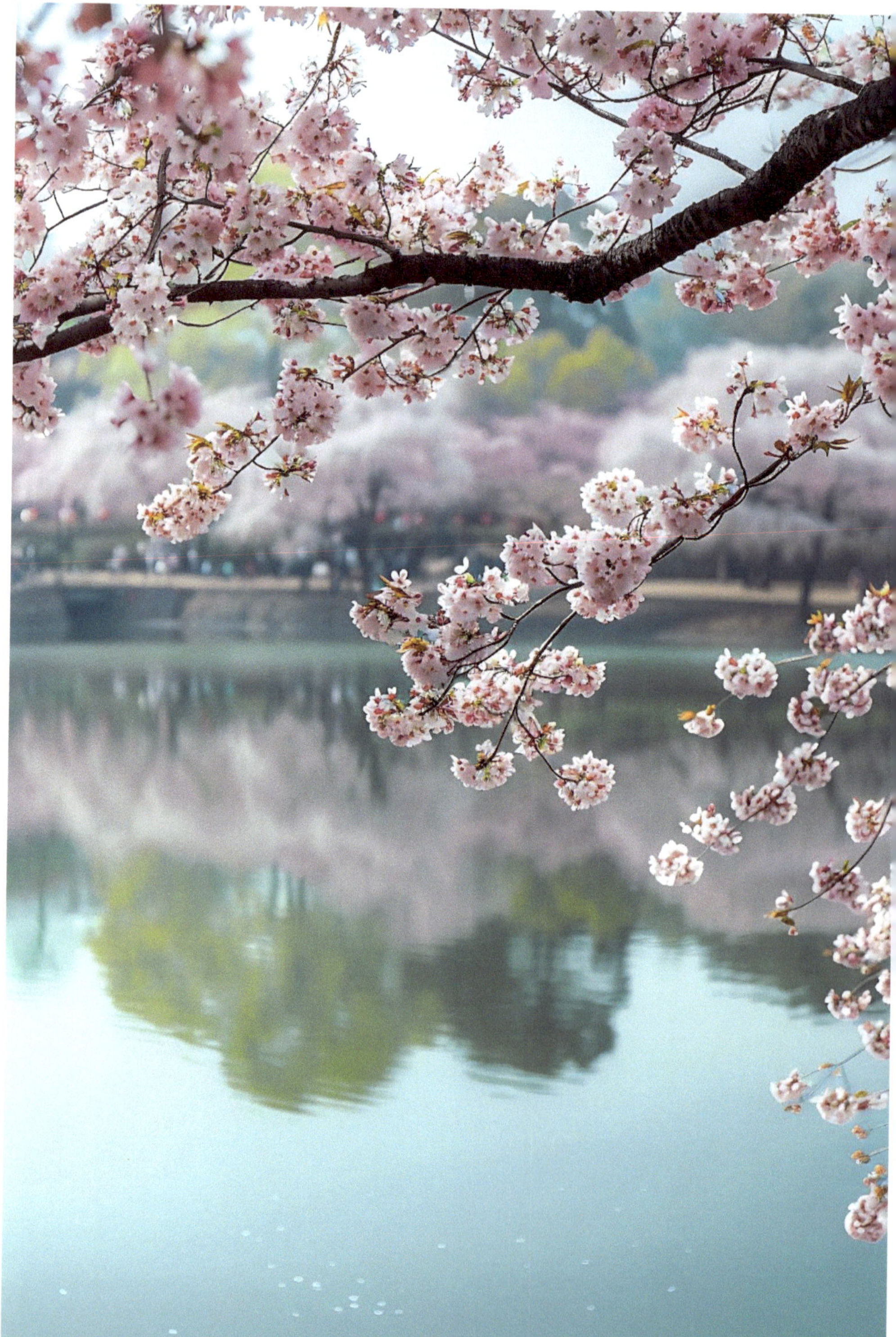

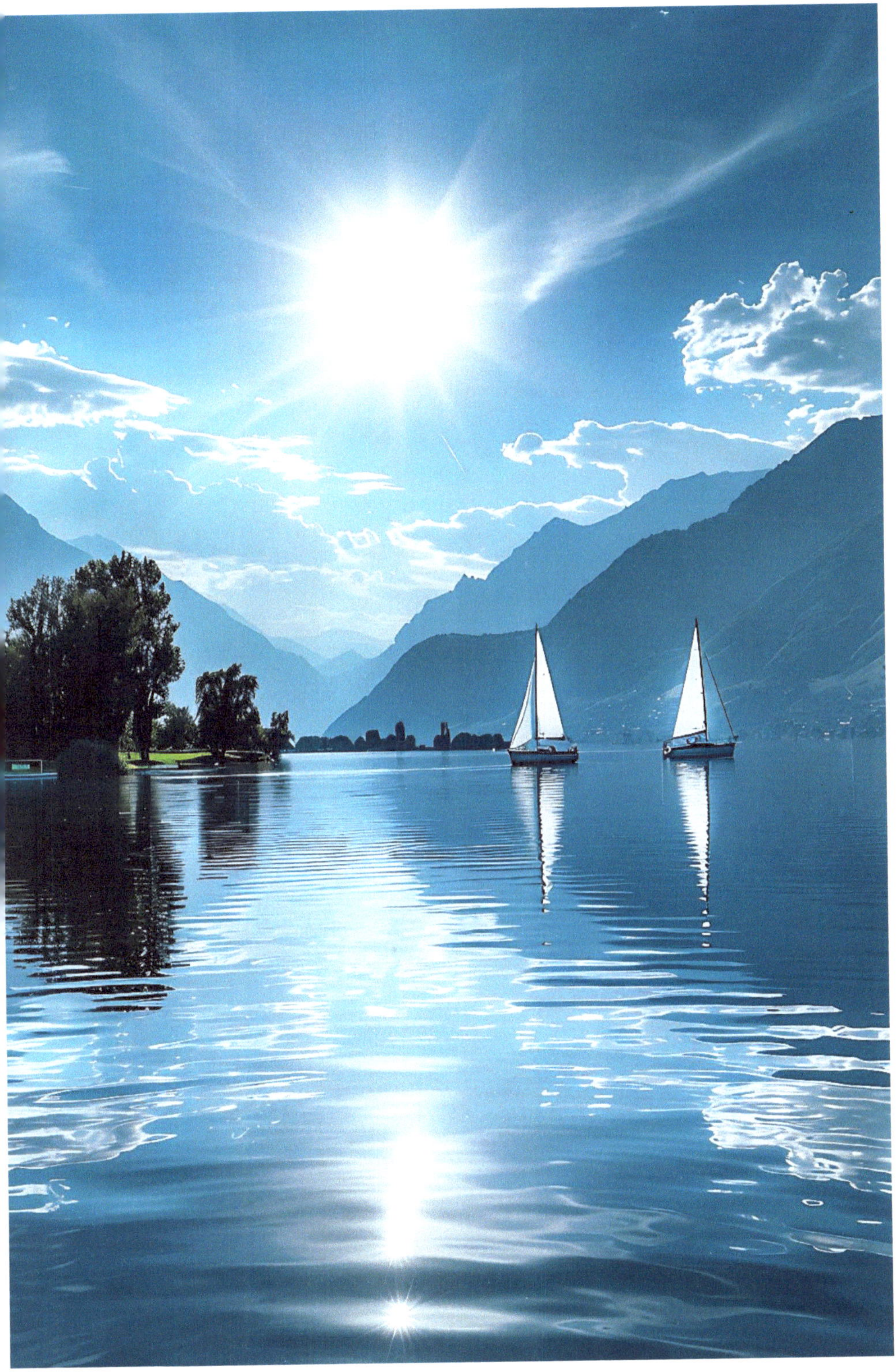

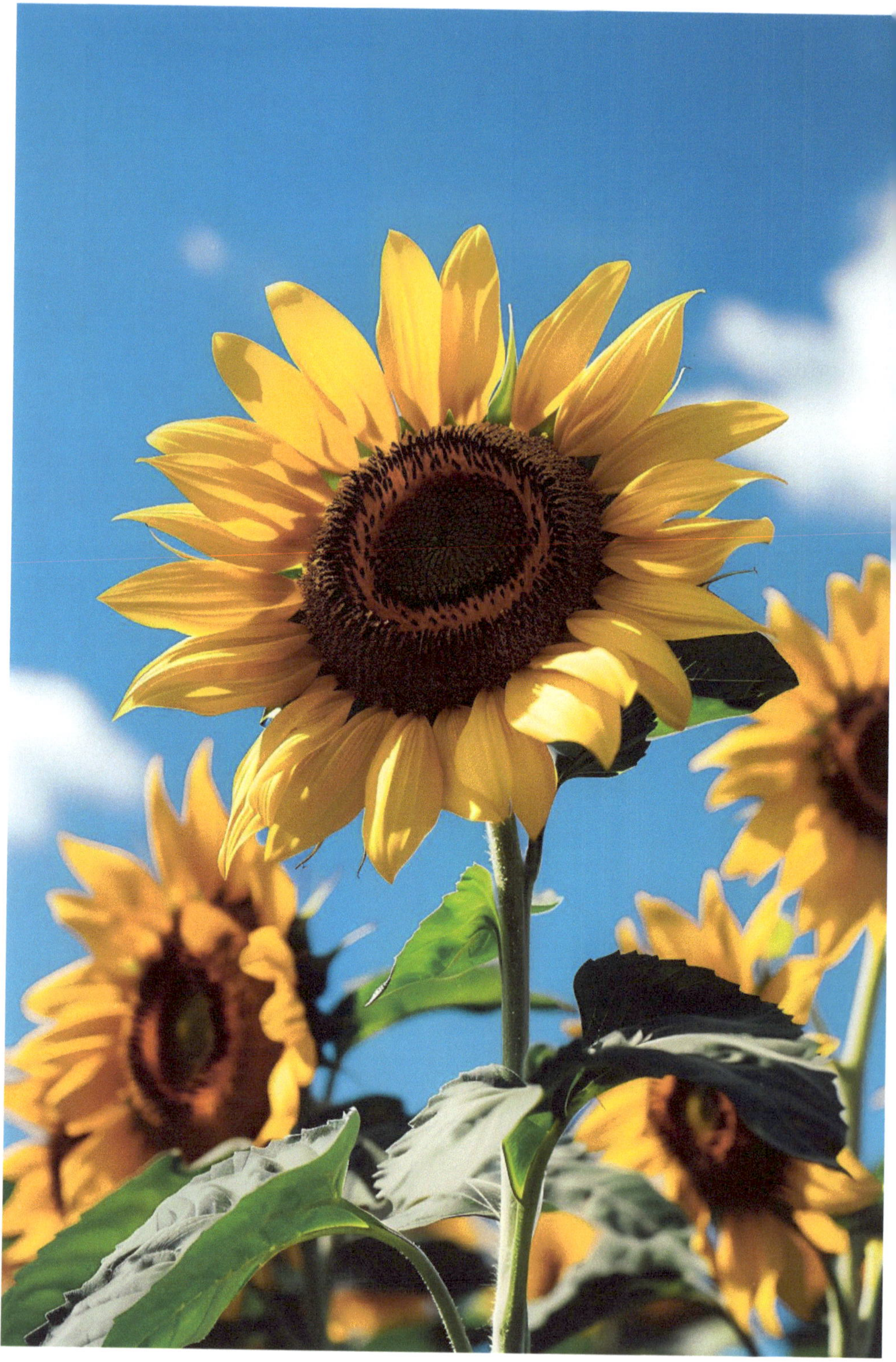

www.ingramcontent.com/pod-product-compliance
Lightning Source LLC
Chambersburg PA
CBHW040759240526
45474CB00008B/113
9798326224712